Muslim Leadership and Women's Education

Muslim Leadership and Women's Education

Uttar Pradesh, 1886–1947

Nasreen Ahmed

Three Essays
COLLECTIVE

First Edition October 2012

ISBN 978-81-88789-91-7

Three Essays
COLLECTIVE

B-957 Palam Vihar, GURGAON (Haryana) 122 017 India
Phone: 91-124 2369023, +91 98681 26587, +91 98683 44843
info@threeessays.com Website: www.threeessays.com
Printed and bound by Glorious Printers, New Delhi

Contents

Editor's Note

My friend Nasreen Ahmad was a student at Aligarh Muslim University during the 1970s, and the basic research which informs this book was done by her between 1975 and 1978, which she subsequently continued with some interruptions. For various reasons she could complete this manuscript only in 2009, shortly before she died bravely fighting cancer.

She was a very warm and pleasant person, a wonderful friend, and outspoken in defense of what she believed in. She was modern in her outlook even in those days and it was natural that she should choose a theme related to women for her research work.

This study, for which she was awarded her Ph.D. posthumously, is a pioneering work and has not been superseded because the material she provides has still not found its way in the few books on the subject of Muslim women's education; mainly because her canvas is larger than gender concerns and focuses on the perceptions of the Muslim intelligentsia as well regarding women in general and women's education in particular. The historical backdrop to Muslim women's education is in fact the strong point of her study.

While studies abound on 'the woman's question' within the social reform movements among other communities, those on social change and 'modernisation' among the Muslims have missed the women; and those on Muslim women have not been concerned with Muslim society in general. Nasreen's study looks at modern education for women in the context of the role of the Muslim leadership of late nineteenth and first half of the twentieth century.

The study is rich in sociological data: she records a great deal that feminist scholars writing on Muslim women today have missed.

We are made privy to the nitty-gritty of building institutions from the scratch, the sources of support and opposition, the efforts to raise resources, how issues and logistics of purdah had to be dealt with, and of getting girls to and from schools. The most interesting details are the social profiles of those involved in promoting women's education and the varying social composition of students in the different ventures – the zenana learning, schools opened by the Christian missionaries and by the Muslim community, the government support/attitude to them. The actors who supported the cause come alive in the pages, we see women playing key roles.

We learn that Sheikh Abdullah, who founded the first girls' school and built it into a college in Aligarh was a convert, a fact that seems not to have mattered even to those who were horrified at his ventures; his wife Begum Waheed Jahan decided to reside in the boarding house with the students; many of the pioneers in women's education were Muslim League members; the Nawab of Rampur opened the maximum number of schools; and various other crucial details.

We see how the trajectory of debates regarding women education parallels in many ways those within other communities, even as it has its own specificities. The study offers much material for comparisons, including how tradition and modernity, reformism and revivalism impinge on women's education: while there was opposition to women's education within a section of the colonial Muslim leadership, many of those who did pioneer women's education were far more enlightened than many others in other communities considered more advanced or 'forward'.

Information such as this book contains could become the basis for further studies on some important related themes of contemporary concern.

Nasreen would have been happy to see her work in print. It has been a joy and remembrance of our association for me to have been a part of this endeavor.

Nalini Taneja

Foreword

This small volume carries an attempt by a young woman to examine the process of modernization of the Indian Muslims in one of its vital aspects, namely imparting of modern education to women. It is an expanded version of her earlier research for the M.Phil. dissertation submitted at the Centre of Advanced Study in History, Aligarh Muslim University, in 1978, and her subsequent Ph.D. thesis for the Purvanchal University, Jaunpur, in 2009.

The author critically evaluates traditionalist attitudes on women's education among Indian Muslims rooted in Islamic theology as well as pre-modern aristocratic culture. She highlights the contrasting attitudes within the Aligarh Movement, from Sir Syed Ahmed Khan onwards, about educating Muslim girls, or establishing girls' schools. She shows how, against a powerful trend opposed to modern education for women, a group of enlightened young men, mostly products of M.A.O. College, endeavoured, from late 1890s onwards, to reorient the Aligarh Movement towards recognizing women's education as one of its objectives. Despite continuing resistance from conservative sections, this trend was successful, by 1938, in securing recognition for the Women's College established by Sheikh Abdullah as a part of the Aligarh Muslim University.

This is a fascinating story which would be of much interest to all those interested in studying the successes as well as failures of the process of modernization among Indian Muslims.

Aligarh

Iqtidar Alam Khan

Preface

There has been a growing concern about the lack of education among Muslims in India. The Census of India 2001, for the first time, gives detailed educational data across religious groups. The findings are disheartening. The study irrefutably establishes that on an average, Muslim men and women are far less educationally accomplished than their non-Muslim counterparts across India. While it is true that average educational levels in India are relatively low, the percentage of 'literate' Muslims – those with elementary reading and writing skills – is much lower than the rest, and the gap widens further up the educational ladder. Nationwide, only 55% of Muslim men are literate as compared to 64.5% non-Muslims and 40.6% Muslim women are literate as compared to 45.9% non-Muslim women. Muslim women fare worse in urban India with just one in 100 being a graduate, against 37 for non-Muslims. The findings of the Sachar Committee have also corroborated this dismal picture. Pervasive and severe gender discrimination is an ugly fact in India and it shows in education. The reasons for this educational backwardness among Muslim women may be many, of which biases in the family, though important, would be only one factor. A proper study of the question of Muslim female education in its historical perspective and efforts made in that direction, especially in the late 19th and the early 20th century, is necessary for understanding the historical roots of this vexed problem.

There are very few studies on Muslim female education and they mainly focus on its sociological aspects. Understanding the historical aspect of education for Muslim women, especially assessing the role of the leading lights in the Muslim reform movement of the late 19th and the early 20th century in education, is a lacuna that needs to be addressed. The role of Muslim leaders in Uttar Pradesh and their contribution in the awakening of the Muslim elite, both male and female, the nature of the problems which they encountered and the manner in which they countered them and went ahead in their mission, is the major thrust of this study.

The early 19th century saw the growth of many elements in Indian society that are seen as characteristics of the modern period in Indian history. The socio-economic changes which broadly justify this view were a result of the action and interaction of various forces. The growth of modern education must also, therefore, be traced within this broad framework. The general approach has been one of emphasis on the 'enlightening' effect of western education. In other words, it is, undoubtedly, the British rule and its concomitant features which gave to modern Indian education – as to all other aspects of social life – its characteristic 19th century dimensions. However, the socio-economic structure within which western education was sought to be introduced, and the aspirations and churnings within Indian society, necessarily determined the form formal education, particularly female education assumed. To look for uniformity or homogeneity in either the aspirations or the forms of response to the British initiatives in this regard is fruitless, as the debates on issues involved in Muslim female education alone bear out.

The general attitude towards women and their position in society is an index of the kind of education a mainly conservative society would permit a woman, as much as the education itself in its impact can become a social force changing their status. This is evident from the fact that the impact of western ideas was felt much later in the sphere of Muslim women's education than in men's education, or even Hindu women's education; just as the changes and reforms in Muslim society in general were preceded by those in Hindu society in general, and even by those amongst Hindu women in particular. In fact, the changes in Muslim women's education coincide primarily with changes in other aspects of their social life.

Another significant point to keep in mind is that all traditionalist attitudes amongst the Muslims were not violently averse to women's education. Unexpectedly, even amongst the most conservative, there was a member of the Deoband School, Maulana Ashraf Ali Thanwi, who favoured institutions imparting 'traditional' education for women, despite his very backward views in general on women. On the other hand, Syed Ahmed Khan, a 'modernist', was opposed to formal education for women: even such education as they did receive at home was to be 'traditional' in character as opposed to that of men which was to be 'modern'. This dichotomy, it must be noticed, was there in spite of his being 'modern'. Formal education in school or education at home, and the content of this education were all matters of debate.

Amongst the various agencies that promoted modern education for Muslim women before the rise of the Aligarh movement, the most important were, therefore, the British Government and the Christian missionaries. The proselytizing efforts of the Christian missionaries were the primary factor for the birth of private enterprise for Muslim female education.

The real impetus to women's education, however, came from the initiatives of the Aligarh Movement as evident from the documents relating to the period available in the Aligarh Muslim University Archives, which have been discussed in some detail in this book. The movement for Muslim women's education began in

Syed Ahmad Khan's lifetime, but became intensified only after his death, and in the 20th century the Aligarh movement went beyond its founder and began promoting imparting of modern education through schools.

The establishment and growth of the Muhammadan Girls' School/College, Aligarh, reflected an effort on the part of Sheikh Abdullah, a pioneer in the field, to identify Muslim women's education with the Aligarh Movement and the Girls' School/ college itself with the M.A.O. College/University. This marked an important stage in the integration of women's education with that of men.

Influenced probably by the reformist tendencies of the Aligarh movement, similar movements for education of Muslim women were taking roots in other places like Agra, Rampur, Allahabad and Lucknow. They were facing the same kind of opposition and challenges as in Aligarh. Efforts of people like Justice Syed Karamat Husain in establishing the Muslim girls' school at Lucknow, as also those of other pioneers in Allahabad, Agra and Rampur, have been discussed in the last chapter, along with the conflicts, inhibitions and prejudices that plagued the Muslim society with regard to female education.

This is a broad study of the efforts at modern education for Muslim women especially with reference to the contribution of the Aligarh Movement. The source material in Urdu relating directly to the theme and having critical importance for my work, have been extensively explored.

The proceedings of the Muhammadan Anglo-Oriental Educational Conferences, the Aligarh Institute Gazettes, biographies of persons connected with Muslim female education as well as M.A.O. College/University, the Education Commission Report of 1882, as well as evidences before the Commission, have been thoroughly studied.

I am indebted to a number of people for their unstinting help and guidance. I must particularly mention Dr. Iqtidar Alam Khan,

(Retd.) Professor of History, Aligarh Muslim University, Aligarh, who has been my inspiration behind this work. I would also like to express my gratitude to my supervisor Dr. Mahendra Pratap Singh whose constant encouragement and guidance helped me complete this study. I must also convey my sincere thanks to Professor S.N.R. Rizvi of Gorakhpur University for providing a broad insight and overview of the study. My warm and deep thanks go to my husband and children. Their abiding faith in me made this study possible. I am also thankful to the library staff of Maulana Azad Library, Aligarh, Sir Syed Academy, Aligarh, National Archives, New Delhi and the U.P. State Archives, Lucknow for their cooperation.

Lucknow

Nasreen Ahmed

CHAPTER I

Muslim Women's Education in the Nineteenth Century

A Study of the Traditionalist Attitudes

Introduction

During the medieval period the educational profile of Muslim women had been no different from that of Hindu women. Education was confined to a very small minority of women, an exception rather than rule, and one has historical references mainly to the educational attainments of individual women rather than classes or sections of women. Education was imparted through *maktabs*/ madrasas, mosques or through private enterprise.[1]

The dissemination of knowledge took the form of discussions between the learned and the novice. Mosques had schools attached to them. These schools were supported by state grants or by landholders or nobles. Primary education was imparted through *maktabs* and the secondary through the madrasas. The majority of the *maktabs* were neither endowed nor patronized by the state. These institutions were left to individual enterprise; they depended upon the charity of noble individuals. In the villages *maktabs* were often attached to mosques and so were madrasas which were institutions of higher learning. *Khanqahs* or shrines of Muslim saints also acted as centres for dispensing knowledge. The *maktabs* were often placed under the guidance of pious and learned maulvis.

Along with the instruction imparted in the *maktabs*, there was the domestic system of instruction, the aims and character of which were almost the same. The house of every Maulvi was an important seat of learning. Students receiving education in the houses of those teachers were provided free board and lodging. Some students who received education either from their fathers in their own homes or in the house of private learned individuals rose to eminence as scholars and writers in different subjects.

In the *maktabs* the students were taught the basics of reading, writing and arithmetic Besides, they had to learn by heart those portions of the Quran that would be necessary to perform their religious functions.[2]

When Muslim children, especially the Muslim princes, attained the age of 4 years, 4 months and 4 days, they were given in charge of teachers who would instruct them in the various arts and sciences, in a ceremonial function known as *Bismillah Khani. Surah-i-Iqra* was read and the child was asked to repeat it.[3]

In general people considered women's education unnecessary, if not positively injurious to society. Young girls were to be prepared for household work. Due to the purdah system education of Muslim women was naturally restricted, and the same was true of Hindu women. There were separate schools for Muslim girls in those days, though some young girls who got education in schools, had to leave school at an early age. In the harems of kings and nobles, some ladies were educated and some of them even won distinction, but the percentage of such educated ladies constituted only a microscopic part of total Muslim women. Those denied the benefits of general education received domestic training in the performance of their household duties.[4]

Girls received their early education usually from parents at home. Except for a few, there existed no separate schools for girls. In their childhood they were taught along with the boys. After a few years they were segregated from the boys and taught in private schools or at home. They were placed under some elderly lady who trained them in cooking, spinning, sewing, weaving and looking after the young. Domestic Science and household duties formed an important part of the curriculum. In the primary stage, the Muslim girls were taught the basics of reading, writing and recitation and the Quran.

Some regular girls' schools for Muslim girls existed in medieval India. When a girl commenced her studies in a *maktab* there was a common practice of writing an *Idi* – generally a verse relating to the most celebrated Muslim festival called *Id* – or a blessing for a girl on a coloured paper called *Zarfishani.* At this time she was made to read the *Zarfishani* to her parents who then gifted her teacher rich presents in a gathering called for the purpose. This was known as the '*Maktab* Ceremony'. There is evidence of these customs and practices being followed in the provincial kingdoms as well.

Girls belonging to Muslim royal families were often educated privately in their homes. Sultan Razia (1236-40) was highly educated. In addition to reading and writing, she learnt the art of riding and the use of arms. Not only was she herself learned, she was also a patron of learning. Instances abound of princesses having been given liberal education during the Mughal period. Gulbadan Begum, daughter of Babur, was considered to be the first 'literary gem' of the Mughal period. Her work *Humayun Nama* is a valuable source of information on the reign of Humayun. She possessed a vast collection of important books in a library of her own.[5]

Akbar's mother Hamida Banu Begum was an educated woman. Salima Sultana, Humayun's niece, commanded a mastery over Persian language and literature. Maham Anaga, the wet nurse of Akbar was a well-educated lady. She founded a college in Delhi. In Akbar's time, ladies of the royal household were given regular instructions by matrons, and some chambers of the royal palace at Fatehpur Sikri were set apart for holding their school.

Nur Jahan, wife of Jehangir, was well versed in Persian and Arabic literature and took an active interest in political and cultural matters. Jahanara Begum, daughter of Shahjahan, was not only a learned and a talented poet but also encouraged writers and learned men by giving them awards and allowances. Jahanara Begum's tutor, Satiunnisa could read the Quran and had a good knowledge of Persian. Mumtaz Mahal, emperor Shahjahan's wife, was well known for her high accomplishments. Zebunnisa Begum, eldest daughter of Aurangzeb, had not only learnt the Quran by heart, but also knew Arabic and Persian. She was also proficient in mathematics, astronomy and other sciences. Zebunnisa founded a literary academy and a library for the use of scholars. Zinat-un-nisa, the younger daughter of Aurangzeb, received a thorough education and became well versed in the doctrines of Faith. She also patronized men of talent and scholarship.[6]

These examples are enough to show that girls and ladies belonging to Muslim royal and noble families in medieval India were given some kind of literary and religious education.

Some Muslim rulers and nobles established schools for girls. Jalal-ud-Din, the Sultan of Hinwar was a pioneer of women's education in the 15th century. Records show the existence of thirteen schools in the capital. Ghiyas-ud-Din Khilji of Malwa (1463-1500) founded a madrasa at Sarangpur to teach arts and crafts to women. Akbar was also interested in women's education. He established a girls' school in his palace in Fatehpur Sikri. From Jafar Sharif's account in *Qanoon-i-Islam* we learn of the existence of many girls' schools in those days even for the middle classes. Many of these were private schools set up in the houses of the rich where elderly ladies taught the Quran, literary works like *Gulistan* and *Bostan* and some books on morals. As an act of piety, some Muslim widows took up the task of giving religious instructions to poor girls and taught them to read the Holy Quran. Though some of the Mughal princesses were highly educated, their education usually came to a standstill after their marriage and that usually took place at an early age. So only a few of them got an opportunity to acquire mastery over language.[7]

Women of the average middle class families had sufficient knowledge in Hindi or Persian or the provincial language, so that they could study the religious scriptures of their faith. Only women belonging to the lower ranks of the society had no education.[8]

Thus it cannot be said that women's education was totally non-existent in India during the medieval period.

Religious Sanction for Muslim Women's Education in the Nineteenth Century

Women's education in the nineteenth century was the result of the modernising effects of British colonialism and the rise of reform movements both among Hindus and Muslims. It is well known that the movement for imparting modern education for Muslim women began much later than similar movements aimed at educating women belonging to other communities. A concerted effort in this direction could start only with the rise of a distinct tendency within the Aligarh Movement espousing the cause of women's education, towards the close of the 19th century. A few Muslim intellectuals of the late nineteenth and early twentieth centuries regarded the spread of female education an essential condition for the overall progress of the nation. In their eyes, widespread illiteracy among Indian women was largely responsible for the backwardness of the country. This late beginning of such a movement, and its slow progress during the first quarter of the twentieth century, was to a very great degree the result of the persisting traditionalist attitude among the common people as well as the elite groups as a dominant trend, which tended to perpetuate the social constraints from which Muslim women suffered. In other words, Muslim conservatism was responsible for the unsatisfactory educational status of Muslim women. A considerable segment of the leadership among the Indian Muslims during the second half of the nineteenth century looked with particular disfavour on any organized effort to enable women to read and write.[9] In taking this attitude, they were influenced not only by the current interpretations of Islamic theology but also by popular prejudices having no sanction, whatsoever, in the Quran or Sunna.

Before going into a detailed discussion of the traditionalist attitudes regarding women's education, it would be appropriate to take note of the theoretical positions stemming from the Quran and the Sunna regarding this matter, and also the situation, as it obtained in this respect in the early Islamic society.

The Prophet is reported to have said, "The seeking of knowledge is obligatory on every Muslim". In another version of the same *hadis,* which is said to be a comparatively less reliable version, the Prophet is quoted as saying that seeking of knowledge is obligatory for women as well.[10] One may quote numerous *hadis* to show the importance laid on the attainment of knowledge in Sunna. A well-known injunction of the Prophet reads: "Let him who is present impart knowledge to him who is absent."[11]

Another *hadis* recorded by Bukhari says: "Knowledge is maintained only through teaching."[12] There are similar *hadis*es recorded by Muslim and Tirmizi as well. One of the pieces recorded by Muslim goes on to say that: "People are like mines of gold and silver, the more excellent of them in the days of ignorance are the more excellent of them in Islam when they attain knowledge."[13] An interesting *hadis* of this type recorded by Tirmizi runs as follows: "He who goes forth in search of knowledge is in the way of Allah till he returns."[14] Although these are not specific to women, it seems that in the early Islamic society imparting of education to all was not only regarded as proper, but spiritual upliftment and improvement of understanding of women were considered necessary for a balanced growth of the society. Islam lays the basis of mass education: education of men as well as women, of children as well as adults. Bukhari informs us that the Prophet had actually fixed a day in the week for imparting instructions to women.[15]

The Prophet is quoted to have said that acquisition of knowledge is incumbent upon all the faithful men as well as women. He pointed towards the importance of education in this way: "Education has its great value for all human beings. It is education which enables its possessors to distinguish what is forbidden and what is not. Really it is our friend in the desert, our society in solitude, our companion when bereft of friends, it guides us to happiness, and it sustains us in misery."[16]

Besides examples of his daughter Fatima Zehra (RA) and his wife Aisha (RA) who were themselves highly educated ladies of their times, other names of ladies of Arabia like Zainab, Hamida, Safiya, Maria and Al-Kalleyyeh deserve special mention.[17]

"A drop of sweat of the brow of a thinker is better than thousand blood drops of the martyr", is a famous Hadith of the Prophet. The Prophet further said: "Attain knowledge from the cradle to the grave" and "Acquire knowledge even if you have to travel to China".[18] The Prophet is said to have once issued orders for release of those prisoners of war who could teach the Muslim children. Hazrat Ali in his book titled *Nehjul Balaghah* emphatically stressed on the significance of knowledge saying that the one who cognizes his self, cognizes his Lord.[19]

It should be recognized that knowledge in the early Islamic society was generally taken to mean possessing the ability of reading and understanding the Quran and other religious books, so that they could perform their duties in the manner prescribed by Islam. From the early history of Islam numerous instances can be cited of women who were treated with great honour and respect because they possessed knowledge of reading and understanding the Quran and other religious books, and also because of the help they rendered so selflessly in the dissemination of this kind of knowledge. Several such instances are quoted by Maulana Ashraf

Ali Thanwi in his book *Bihishti Zewar.* It would appear from the biographical notices given by Maulana Ashraf Ali Thanwi that, in the early Islamic society, women belonging to different strata could get an opportunity to acquire knowledge and become proficient in reading and interpreting the Quran and Sunna. Few such examples, as cited by Maulana Ashraf Ali Thanwi, relate to the slave girls of Imam Yazid-bin-Haroun and Ibn Simak Kufi, as also Qazi zada Rumi's sister and Imam Rabi'at-ur-Rai's mother. The slave girl of Yazid-bin-Haroun read out to him passages from the Quran when he was unable to read them personally because of his weak eyesight. One of Ibn Simak Kufi's slave girls was also very learned. Maulana Ashraf Ali Thanwi praises them highly for their learning, and comments that the slave girls of those days were highly learned as against the illiterate ladies of his own time.[20] The mother of Imam Rabi'at-ur-Rai and Qazizada Rumi's sister are also mentioned in laudatory words for their unselfish devotion to the dissemination of knowledge.

The great emphasis that has been laid on the education of men as well as women in Islamic thought has often acted as a rejuvenating influence tending towards a partial rejection of the popular prejudices over this question. This process appears to be at work within the Muslim traditional society of the nineteenth century as well.

From a perusal of the writings of the traditionalist ulema of late nineteenth century and early twentieth century, and references to their views in the speeches and writings of their modernist contemporaries, one may gather that, in contravention of the popular traditionalist notion regarding women's education as a source of evil, there was growing a more 'enlightened' trend within the traditionalist framework. This 'enlightened' trend was opposed to the total exclusion of women from education. One strain of this trend, which was more prominent during the second half of the nineteenth century, regarded with disfavor the idea of Muslim girls attending schools, even if these were exclusively women's schools, but strongly supported the imparting of knowledge to them within the families by senior ladies of the community. There was, however, developing, yet another and a more 'radical' strain within the above 'enlightened' trend which favoured the establishment of schools for the education of women, though, perhaps, the school, thus visualized, would be exclusively for Muslim girls. This tendency would become particularly noticeable in the early decades of the twentieth century, when the traditionalists gradually began to think that the stemming of 'modernist' influences spreading from Aligarh, and for maintaining their own ideological and political base among the Muslims, they needed to bring about some changes in their own thinking and approach to social and economic problems.

As mentioned, the more conservative elements within the traditionalist circles, who advocated the total denial of education for women, were guided by certain prejudices and notions existing in the society then. We have a reference to such attitudes in the context of a discussion on the social outlook of Badruddin Tyabji's father, wherein it is mentioned that he did not agree with the people who believe "that it was imprudent and unwise to educate women, as education made them independent and assertive and opened the door to the indiscriminate reading of novels of all kinds and the writing of love letters."[21] Again we come across references to the prevalence of such an attitude from a model letter composed by Maulana Ashraf Ali Thanwi as to how a mother should write to her daughter. In this letter, Maulana Ashraf Ali Thanwi makes a critical reference to such mothers who think that only knowledge of cooking and embroidery is sufficient for girls. [22] We can take this to mean that as late as the beginning of the twentieth century, in many of the '*Ashraf*' families, for whose guidance Maulana Ashraf Ali Thanwi compiled the book that contains the above letter, acquiring any kind of knowledge (like reading and writing), other than cooking and embroidery by their women was regarded as improper. Going beyond the reading of the Quran and a smattering of the Urdu language was considered a dangerous innovation.[23] The spread of female education was regarded as harmful for the society and many intellectuals of the period were vehemently opposing it. The impact of such an attitude on the mentality of Indian women can be gauged from the following excerpt:

> Men succeeded so amazingly in their efforts that they were able to inculcate deeply into the minds of women the conviction that to desire knowledge was neither dignified nor virtuous. They became incapable of aspiring even to learn to read and write. Most women would have been heartily ashamed of an accusation that they were hankering after these very elementals of knowledge and hotly resented it.[24]

As against this attitude of total denial of education to Muslim women, there was growing amongst a section of the Muslim traditionalists of the nineteenth century, a trend that espoused the cause of women's education. But even this new trend was totally opposed to the establishment of schools for the girls. The existence of such a comparatively 'enlightened' tendency in the last quarter of the nineteenth century is borne out by the speeches and writings of Syed Ahmad Khan.[25] It was thought by them that the girls would become bad mannered and irreligious if they attended schools, although they approved of some sort of an indigenous education to be given to girls at home. It seems Syed Ahmad himself subscribed to this view, as evident from his famous Gurdaspur speech of 1884.[26] Mrs. Meer Hasan Ali in her book *Observations on the Mussalmauns of India* also does not mention anything regarding the system of sending girls to schools. Most probably, such a system was looked down upon in the polite society described by her. But at the same time it should be noted that in the social groups in which Mrs. Meer Hasan Ali moved, the Lucknow of the mid-nineteenth century, the education of girls was looked upon as a desired pursuit. There was, according to her, a demand for educated girls in the marriage market of the upper classes. In fact she mentions that the men in the family thought it to be their duty to instruct 'the female under their charge'[27] In any case, owing to absence of an elaborate system of education for women, the number of educated girls or even those with a knowledge of arts like stitching, weaving and embroidery, which were considered added qualifications was quite limited.[28]

The model curriculum for women in the eighteenth and early part of the nineteenth century Awadh was the teaching of *Bughdadi Qayadah* followed by the knowledge of how to read and write. Emphasis was on cramming. Apart from teaching Arabic and Persian, they were also taught mathematics, grammar and the art of letter writing. Under religious education, they were taught the holy Quran, *Hadis* and *Gulistan, Bostan*. In the later days, when Urdu flourished, Urdu *qayadah* was also included in the curriculum.[29]

The more radical elements within this 'enlightened' group of traditionalists were favourably disposed towards the establishment of schools for Muslim girls, provided due attention was given to the strict observance of the purdah and the teaching of religious books together with other subjects like arithmetic, domestic science and Urdu. They were not in favour of adopting western education for Indian girls and had presented their own ideal form of female education, which contained "the essence of the traditional Indian, social, religious, ethical and cultural values."[30]

Their love and passion for their own religion and culture and their concern to preserve the traditional morality of their women persuaded them to advocate an emphasis on these values.[31] A leaning of this kind is discernable in the attitude of no less a person than Maulana Ashraf Ali Thanwi, who can, by all counts, be regarded as the most representative spokesperson of the orthodox traditionalism that was being fostered at Dar'ul Ulum of Deoband. *Bihishti Zewar* (Heavenly Ornaments) is a lengthy multi-volume instructional guidebook written by Thanwi and published probably in 1911. Aimed at female readership, *Bihishti Zewar* was intended to instruct Muslim girls and women in religious teachings, proper behaviour and prudent conduct. It was intended to provide young women with all they needed to know on how to run their own lives as well as those of their families. Yet Thanwi, like other contemporary writers on the subject of female education, was almost revolutionary in his insistence that women in purdah should be educated (in schools) like their menfolk.

Writing in 1911, Maulana Ashraf Ali Thanwi mentions in his preface of the help rendered towards the publication of his book *Bihishti Zewar* by a manager of a girls' school. This shows that he was not averse to such institutions for girls[32] and did not see any difficulty in associating with such institutions, provided the nature of the education imparted in these schools was religious and traditional.[33]

In his biographical notices of early Islamic women, he singles out for special praise those women who were well known for their culture and learning, and advises women of his own time to likewise attain such literary achievements.[34] The height of education or knowledge, according to him, was to be able to read and understand the *Quran*. In his model composition of a letter from a mother to a daughter, Maulana Ashraf Ali Thanwi gives us a clear picture of his views on the nature of education for girls. In this letter he disapproves of the attitude of those mothers who think that knowledge of sewing and embroidery and cooking is enough for girls. According to him, this kind of attitude is born of ignorance. He deems it necessary for every woman to at least know how to read and write Urdu, as a lot of benefits are expected to accrue to the girls from such knowledge. The pronunciation improves, and by the study of good books on religion one becomes conscious of the do's and don'ts of religion. By being learned and aware of one's religion, one can avoid committing acts that go against religion. The domestic economy runs smoothly if the housewife is educated. An educated woman is more particular about the proper upbringing of her children. She will talk and behave, in the presence of children, in a decent manner that will have a good effect on them, and they would emulate her qualities. An educated woman would know how to treat her parents, husband and other relatives with respect. Also, if a woman knows how to read and write, she will not face any difficulties in writing to her relatives and conveying her personal and innermost feelings. In the absence of proper education she will be helpless and would have to take the help of an outsider in corresponding with her relatives which, in turn, would result in the outsider coming to know of her private affairs.[35]

Maulana Ashraf Ali Thanwi then goes on to describe in detail as to the ways in which this knowledge could be acquired. He lays down three steps for the same. Firstly, he thinks that it is necessary for girls to read Persian books and then to proceed to read Arabic books. He finds no language, other than Arabic, to be conducive for promoting religious education. He then prescribes *Taisir'ul Mubtadi*, written by a friend of his, Abdullah Maulvi, to be read when a basic knowledge of Arabic is gained. Early coaching on these lines for three years would make the girls proficient in Arabic enabling them to talk with confidence about subjects relating to the *Quran* and *Hadis*. Secondly, he advises Muslim girls to clear their doubts regarding basic faith with the help of someone well versed in Islamic religion. Thirdly, he suggests to them to read books in Urdu about Islam with the help of a competent teacher. He then mentions a number of books that are supposed to have good or ill effects on the girls. Some of the good books mentioned are:

1. *Tafsir-e-Qadiri*
2. *Tarjuma Tafsir-e-Hussaini*
3. *Tarjuma Mashariq-a-Qul-Anwar*
4. *Saliqa Tarjuma Adab'ul Mufrad*
5. *Salat ur Rahman*
6. *Rah-e-Najat*

7. *Nasihat'ul Muslimin.*
8. *Sa'adat Darain*
9. *Bihisht ka Darwaza*
10. *Haqeeqat'ul Salat*
11. *Risala Tajhiz-wa Takfin*
12. *Kashf ul Hajat*
13. *Safai-Mu'amalat*
14. *Tamiz'ul Kalam*
15. *Mahasin'ul Amal.*
16. *Hidayat'ul Niswan.*
17. *Tehzib-e Niswan-wa Tarbiyat'ul Insan*
18. *Ta'li-un-Nisama*
19. *Jehad-e-Akbar*
20. *Ghaza-e-Ruh*
21. *Chashma-e-Rehmat*
22. *Gulzar-e-Ibrahim.*

Some of the books, which, according to Maulana Ashraf Ali Thanwi, are likely to have an evil effect on girls, and which therefore girls needed to be kept away from, were as follows:

1. Collected works of poets in general and collections of ghazals in particular.
2. *Inder Sabha*
3. *Quissa Badr-e-Munir*
4. *Dastan-e-Amir Hamza*
5. *Alif Laila'*
6. *Falnama*
7. *Arayish-e-Mahfil*
8. *Tafsir Sura-e-Yusuf*
9. Novels

The effect of novels on girls, according to him, is like the effect of poison.[36]

An analysis of the type of books prescribed for reading shows that secular education had no place in the traditional system of education for Muslim girls.

Much emphasis was laid on imparting religious education and on teaching the girls good behaviour and house management. The Muslim girls were expected to read and write only that much as would enable them to write letters and keep an account of the household expenditure, and also learn some art or craft so that, when the need arose, they could earn something by dint of their labour.[37]

It is significant that the kind of education for girls prescribed by Maulana Ashraf Ali Thanwi is more or less the same as depicted by Mrs. Meer Hasan Ali in her book, *Observations on the Mussalmauns of India*, first published in 1832. Writing about the way of life of the *ashraf* of the early nineteenth century, she observes that, the women, despite living in seclusion and not having the benefit of secular education, were aware of their moral duties and were extremely refined in their behaviour[38] – the two qualities that Maulana Ashraf Ali Thanwi would like girls to acquire through the reading of religious and other 'good' books. Mrs. Meer Hasan Ali observes: "Women are devout in their prayers and strict in their observance of ordinances."[39] They were instructed in their religious doctrines by the men of the family.[40] In Syed families, the children of both sexes were taught from early childhood to recount their pedigree up to Hasan or Hussain.[41] At another place she remarks that the Muslim women of the *zenana* appeared to her as "obedient wives, dutiful daughters, affectionate mothers, kind mistresses, sincere friends and liberal benefactresses to the distressed poor."[42]

They were gifted with good sense and politeness, were shrewd in their remarks, and their language was correct and refined, because the men with whom the women conversed were generally well educated.[43] This goes on to show that in the case of Muslim women belonging to *ashraf* families of the nineteenth century, absence of formal education was seen as adequately compensated for by impeccable upbringing and grooming. However, the proficiency to read and write Arabic, Persian and Urdu that Maulana Ashraf

Ali Thanwi considers to be an essential part of a girl's education was acquired by a very limited number of Muslim women.

From the reports of discussions that took place at the annual sessions of the Mohammadan Educational Congress from 1886 onwards regarding the problem of women's education, the picture that emerges of the situation within the Muslim traditional society in this respect is almost identical with that depicted by Mrs. Meer Hasan Ali and Maulana Ashraf Ali Thanwi. But the information gleaned from the reports of these discussions certainly adds a new dimension to our understanding of the situation in so far as these are focused on the negative attitude that the traditionalists of different hues had towards the schools for girls established by the official agencies. The reports also bring to our notice the practical difficulties of arranging private tutoring for girls.

Thomas R. Metcalf in his book *Land, Landlords and the British Raj* writes that the taluqdars' interest in education in the late eighteenth and the early nineteenth centuries was 'fitful, sporadic and often conspicuous, designed to show the British that they were an enlightened aristocracy'.[44] Those who founded schools comprised but a small number of taluqdars and they were not interested in the dissemination of learning, but instead, they wanted to be known as 'beneficent aristocrats'.[45]

The Colvin Taluqdars School established in 1890, primarily to educate the wards and children of the taluqdars, faced difficulties in student enrolment. Though the government put pressure on the 'recalcitrant' taluqdars to send their sons, the parents of only seventeen out of sixty-seven eligible boys, were willing to enrol their sons. The rest were either wholly uninterested in the scheme, or else cowed down by 'zenana influence',[46] giving in to the wishes of the Rani who did not want them to part with their sons. The influential Raja of Mahmudabad, Amir Hasan Khan, who was made to promise to send his two teen-aged sons to the school, did not keep his promise. The boys of the taluqdar of Oel left for home without leave after attending school for only a day, because "the Rani had sent two telegrams recalling them."[47]

From the above mentioned examples it seems that education of the boys of even the taluqdars was not a priority. At a time when education for even Muslim boys was in its infancy, education for Muslim girls could find no mention in the agenda of the Muslim '*ashraf*' class. Moreover, socialization ensured that women proved to be impediments in the spread of education even of boys, if it were to be through schools. They could, therefore, hardly be expected to favour sending their daughters outside the home to attend schools.

From a perusal of the data collected for the guidance of the Mohammadan Educational Conference on the issue of women's education, and the speeches delivered at the sessions of the Conference, one gathers that the number of Muslim girls attending the girls' schools established by the official agencies was negligible, and also that, it was only in the Punjab that in certain districts a few Muslims did send their girls to the schools, but in most cases these were institutions where only pupils coming from Muslim families would study. These schools were apparently located in predominantly Muslim villages and towns. There are also a few references to the schools for Muslim girls run by private organizations, but all such schools were basically meant for imparting religious education. One such institution appears to have existed at Jabalpur in the eighties. But the most widely prevalent pattern of education was no doubt the traditional one under which, in most of the 'respectable' families, girls were taught by elderly women teachers.[48] The method most probably followed was that a 'refined', 'educated', and 'capable' lady of the *mohalla* was entrusted with teaching the elementary books and faith to the 'purdah-clad' and 'decent' girls of the locality by way of favour.[49] Such a voluntary lady teacher would also give lessons in domestic arts like stitching, cooking, etc. The beneficial effects of this kind of education and the good influence of the lady teacher, who herself would be a 'decent, honest and good hearted' person would help the girls to improve themselves, contributing to "making thousands of homes happy and honest".[50] It is, however, maintained that this pattern of education had one serious drawback. The kind of lady teachers who would be considered fit for running a tutoring center in their homes were difficult to find. It was particularly difficult to find a tutor who in addition to proficiency in reading *Quran* should also have sufficient knowledge of Persian and Urdu. This situation would sometimes force more well-to-do and 'enlightened' parents to hire lady teachers for tutoring their daughters at their own homes. In certain cases this tutoring was done by the male members of the family.[51]

Thus it can be seen that in the nineteenth and the early twentieth century, education of Muslim women was not given much importance. In the Muslim society, apparently, female education was not considered an important prerequisite for the overall progress of the community. A close examination of the attitude of the traditionalist sections of the community over this issue brings forth three distinct strains of opinion:

- The outright denial of education to women
- Favouring a particular kind of religious education for girls to be imparted at home.
- Favouring education exclusively through schools.

There was almost near unanimity between the last two tendencies on the point that secular education should have only a minimal place in the curriculum. In advocating these opinions the traditionalists mainly depended on the particular interpretations that they would seek to give to the *hadis* and the Quranic injunctions with respect to women's position in the society.

Education of girls in the Muslim traditionalist society in the nineteenth century was very meagre, firstly because there were very few schools for Muslim girls, and secondly because it was difficult to find educated women who could teach the girls at home. It was only with the rise of the Aligarh Movement that some sort of concrete efforts were directed towards Muslim women's education. That these efforts met with stiff opposition from a large section of people involved in the Aligarh Movement who had the powerful backing of no less a person than Syed Ahmad Khan himself is a different story.

References and Notes

1. Sharma, S. Ram, *Women and Education: Women's Education in Ancient and Muslim Period,* Vol. II, Discovery Publishing House, 1995, p. 47. See also Jaffer, S.M., *Education in Muslim India (1000-1800)* Idarah-i-Adabiyat-i Delli, 1973, pp. 187-198.

   While madrasas provided education (religious and/or regular), *maktabs* were neighbourhood schools, often attached to mosques that provided religious education to children who attended other schools to get 'mainstream' education.

2. Ibid., p. 48.
3. Ibid., p. 49.
4. Ibid., p. 87. See also Mathur, Y.B., *Women's Education in India 1813-1966,* Asia Publishing House, New Delhi, p.3.
5. Ibid., p. 87. See also Jaffer, S.M., op. cit., pp.187-198.
6. Ibid., pp. 88-89.
7. Ibid., p. 90.
8. Ibid., p. 91.
9. Tyabji, Hussain B. *Badruddin Tyabji, a Biography,* Thacker & Co., Bombay, 1952, p. 10. Badruddin Tyabji's father, Tyab Ali (born in 1903) discarded the current notion that education would make the girls 'independent' and 'assertive' and lead to the reading of novels and writing of love letters.
10. *A Manual of Hadith,* edited by Maulana Muhammad Ali, The Ahmadiya Anjuman Tah'aat Islam, Lahore, p. 39. It should, however,

be noted, that the more authentic *hadis*, quoted above, also makes it obligatory upon all Muslims, men as well as women, to acquire knowledge.

11. Ibid., Bukhari, 3:37, cited by Maulana Muhammad Ali, *A Manual of Hadith*, p. 33.
12. Ibid., Bukhari, 3:10, p. 38.
13. Ibid., Muslim, 2:1, p. 37.
14. Ibid., Tirmizi, 39:2, p. 38.
15. Ibid., Bukhari, 3:35, p. 34. The Prophet himself made arrangements for the education of women: "The women said to the Prophet, – the men have got an advantage over us in approaching thee, therefore, appoint for us a day from thy self; so he promised them a day in which he met them and he exhorted them and gave them commandments."
16. Kauser, Zeenat, *Muslim Women in Medieval India*, Janaki Prakashan, Patna, 1992, p. 139.
17. Ibid.
18. Jafri, Maqsood, 'Islamic Concept of Education', *Muslim Youth*, February 2006, Vol. XIX. Issue 142.
19. Ibid.
20. Thanwi, Maulana Ashraf Ali, *Bihishti Zewar*, Madina Book Depot, Delhi, Part 8, pp. 493-4. The date of the publication of the book is not mentioned. However, we can gauge the approximate date of publication by the date mentioned at the end of the preface to the book, 1332 Hijri, corresponding to approximately 1911.
21. Tyabji, op. cit., p.10.
22. Thanwi, op. cit., Part I, pp. 17-19.
23. Nawab Sultan Jahan Begum, *An Account of My Life*, Vol. II, translated by C.H. Payne, The Times Press, Bombay, 1927, Vol. III, p. 323.
24. Hausewirth, Frieda, *Purdah: The Status of Indian Women*, p.96, London, 1932.
25. *Mohammadan Educational Congress*, 1888. Speech by Syed Ahmad Khan, p. 118. The Conference began under the title, 'Muhammadan Educational Congress' in 1886. In 1890 this was changed to 'Muhammadan Educational Conference' (Resolution No. 1, 5th Session)

and again in 1895, the title was changed to Muhammadan Anglo-Oriental Educational Conference' (Resolution No. 3, 10th Session).

26. *Saiyid Ahmad Khan Ka Safar Nama-e-Punjab,* edited by Moulvi Syed Iqbal Ali, Aligarh Institute Press, 1884, p. 103.
27. Ali, Mrs. Meer Hasan, *Observations on the Mussulmauns of India,* Idarah-i-Adabiyat-i-Delhi, 1973, Vol. I, p. 176.
28. Ibid., p. 9
29. Rehana Begum, *Oudh ke Samajik Jeevan ka Itihas (1720-1819),* p. 140, Delhi, 1994.
30. Jaswal, G.M., 'The Model Curriculum for Women Formulated by the Muslim Intelligentsia of the Pre-Gandhian Era' *Proceedings of the Indian History Congress,* Session Delhi University, December 2007.
31. Ibid.
32. Thanwi, op. cit., Part 1, p. 5.
33. Ibid. Part 10, pp. 673-74.
34. Ibid., Part 8, pp. 494-495.These examples give us an idea of the author's concept of a very learned person. Having a good knowledge of religion was supposed to be the height of knowledge anyone could attain.

    Qazi Zada Rumi's sister hid her jewels in her brother's luggage when he went to Rum (Turkey) to acquire knowledge, so that these would be handy whenever he needed money for financing his studies. When Imam Rabi's father went for war, he gave 30,000 *'ashrafis'* to his wife and his wife spent all the money on the education of her son, Imam Rabi'at ur Rai, who became a very learned person and taught *hadis* in a mosque.
35. Ibid., Part 1, pp. 17-18.
36. Ibid., Part 19, pp. 673-74. It is significant to note that the list of books condemned by Thanwi included *Tafsir Sura-I-Yusuf.* This goes to suggest that he would consider any kind of love story, even the one contained in the Quran, as unsuitable for reading by girls. Maulana Ashraf Ali Thanwi seems to proceed on the assumption that any creative writing depicting human relationships in an intimate manner would have a bad effect on the moral outlook of a girl.
37. Ibid., Part 5, p. 307.
38. Ali, op. cit., Vol. I, p. 176.

39. Ibid., Vol. I, p. 176.
40. Ibid., Vol. I, p. 176.
41. Ibid., Vol. I, p. 6.
42. Ibid., Vol. I, p. 313.
43. Ibid., Vol. I, p. 113.
44. Metcalf, R. Thomas, *Land, Landlords and the British Raj – Northern India in the Nineteenth Century*, Oxford University Press, Delhi, 1979, p. 318.
45. Ibid., p. 319.
46. Ibid., p. 322.
47. Ibid., p. 323.
48. Muhammadan Educational Congress, 1886, p. 11.
49. Ibid., 1888, p. 110. Speech by Sheikh Khairuddin.
50. Ibid.
51. Ibid., District Hoshiarpur.

Chapter II

Efforts for the Education of Muslim Women, 1857-1885

During the 19th century, Muslim women's education in India was fostered by three different agencies, the government, missionaries and 'Native' enterprise. Of these agencies, to begin with, the most important contribution was that of the British administration. But in this connection, it should be remembered that British administration did not formulate a separate policy for the education of Muslim women. A study of the British educational policy regarding female education in general becomes necessary to gauge its impact with respect to Muslims.

Over the course of the 19th century, the former indigenous system of schooling in British India was largely replaced by the new state system of education introduced formally by the East India Company in 1854 and developed by the British crown after 1857. Under the former indigenous system, schools were of two types – elite religious schools geared towards students interested in a lifetime of higher learning, and local elementary schools where village boys were introduced to the 3R's in the vernacular medium. These schools were common in many parts of the country and approximately 8% to 12% of the male population was literate while women and lower castes were generally illiterate.[1]

The government did not recognize female education as a branch of state system of education before the receipt of the Dispatch of 1854 from the Court of Directors. The attention of the authorities does not appear to have been directed to the subject until many years after they had adopted definite measures for the education of boys.[2] Barring an extremely small number of women, who received some rudimentary education, either at home or at schools, general or special, almost the whole of the female population of the country was deprived of formal education till 1854. Prior to that date, the education of girls, it seems, was left entirely in the hands of individuals and private societies, "for in none of the general Dispatches relating to educational matters submitted to or received from the Court of Directors during the first half of the 19th century, is there any reference to the education of girls or women."[3] The problem that faced British officials was, whether the East India Company should do anything to promote education among the women of India. The conservatives among them refused to have anything to do with the subject. They pointed out that the policy of the Company was one of strict social and religious neutrality; that the prejudices against the education of women which prevailed among the people were so strongly rooted in their social and religious life that any attempt to educate women would create a very great commotion. It seems that the authorities both in England and in India were of the opinion that any attempt to introduce female education, when there was no demand for it, might be regarded by the people as interference with their social customs[4] and that the efforts of the administration should be restricted to the education of men, who would themselves at a later date, undertake the education of their women folk.

The credit for having brought about a change in this conservative view goes to Lord Dalhousie. Dalhousie decided that the open patronage of Government should be extended to the education of women.[5] The following extract from his Order dated 11th April 1850, gives an indication of his views on the subject.

> It is the opinion of the Governor-General in Council that no single change in the habits of the people is likely to lead to more important and beneficial consequences than the introduction of education for their female children. The Governor-General in Council requests that the Council of Education may be informed that it is hence forward to consider its functions as comprising the superintendence of native female education, and that wherever any disposition is shown by the natives to establish female schools it will be its duty to give them all possible encouragement and further their plans in every way that is not inconsistent with the efficiency of the institutions already under their management.'[6]

This view was later confirmed by the Dispatch of 1854.With regard to female education, the Dispatch observed:

> The importance of female education in India cannot be overrated; and we have observed with pleasure the evidence which is now afforded of an increased desire on the part of many of the natives of India to give a good education to their daughters. By this means, a far greater proportional impulse is imparted to the educational and moral tone of the people than by the education of men. We have already observed that female schools are included among those to which grants-in-aid may be given; and we cannot refrain from expressing our cordial sympathy with the efforts which are being made in this direction. Our Governor-General in Council has declared in a communication to the government of Bengal that the Government ought to give to the native female education in India its frank and cordial support.[7]

Contrary to the belief of Dalhousie and other officials serving under him that their policy of female education was popular among the Indians and that there was an increased desire among the people to send their girls to schools, the policy initiated by him was not liked by various sections of the people. It was especially unpopular among the Muslims. The only exception in this respect was a very small number of people who belonged to the non-Muslim upper class. This is for instance apparent from a write up that appeared in a Lucknow based Urdu weekly *Talism*[8] published by certain circles critical of the British administration established after the annexation of Awadh. Incidentally, this write up also goes to testify that this policy was being implemented uniformly all over the British territories. The paper says: 'In every Northern and Western district schools have been established and strict orders have been issued for the education of girls.' We are informed that in the districts of Agra and Mathura, twelve schools for the education of girls were opened and girls from leading Kayastha and Brahmin families attended these schools. There is also mention of government sanctioning an annual grant of Rs.326, possibly for establishing a school for girls in the newly annexed territory of Awadh. A closer scrutiny of this seemingly innocent write-up shows that in the estimate of the editors of *Talism* the British administration's policy of encouraging female education was bound to be unpopular with the people, and they were ready to use it for creating public opinion against the new regime in Awadh. While ostensibly praising British efforts for female education, the write-up also contains the following sneering statements: 'Now women will take lead over men. They would put to shame the intelligent people by quoting to them from *Bahar-i-Danish*. Those who did not know to distinguish between *Alif* and *Be* would thus become professors (*allama*). By studying in these schools, they would obliterate the pride and contribution of so many people.'

The fact that this write-up appeared just two weeks before the outbreak of the Rebellion of 1857 shows that British government's policy with respect to female education might also have been one of the issues over which popular resentment was sought to be built up by those opposed to British rule.

After the Rebellion of 1857 the government was reluctant to get directly involved in female education on grounds that government efforts in this area might excite religious and political opposition. The repression after 1857 was accompanied by an emphatic declaration of a policy of social and religious neutrality by the Queen. Lord Stanley, in his Dispatch of 1859, observed that both the difficulties and the importance of female education are adequately appreciated by the officers of the Department of Education, and invited the views of the Governor-General in Council as to the nature and degree of the influence which may safely and properly be exerted by the officers of the Department of Education to promote the extension of schools of females.[9]

The problem before the government regarding female education was of a delicate nature. When the vocal sections among people were not yet ready to accept the education of their womenfolk, they would least tolerate interference from the Government towards furthering that cause.

At least in so far as the Muslim upper classes were concerned, they were totally opposed to the Government's intervention to promote female education. Even those among them who had a reputation for liberal and pro-administration leanings were not prepared to support the revival of the policy enunciated in the Woods Dispatch of 1854.The Scientific Society of Syed Ahmad Khan[10] contended in 1868 that the state abstain from meddling with female education and considered active interference on the part of the Government not only impolitic, but even dangerous, which would arouse suspicion against and retard the progress of an independent movement for women's education They believed that such a movement, if left to itself, will be successful, provided the initiative was taken by the 'Natives'.[11] In other words, what they wanted was that the Government should trust solely to private enterprise for the success of the female educational scheme, or else the movement for female education would be simply retarded. if not rendered hopeless, by direct interference.[12]

The Government's educational policy was, therefore, not one of direct 'interference'. Its support was conditional on the spontaneous impulse of the people in favour of female education. It was open to all local authorities, whether district officials or of the Education Department, to stimulate a desire or at least a willingness to accept female education, and it was intended that when such genuine desire was forthcoming, the Government would come forward and liberally support it.[13]

The British Government played an important role in furthering 'Native Female Education' in the shape of granting funds and convincing people of the need and importance of female education. In the speech delivered in the Shahjahanpur Institute[14] on 19 December 1868 the Lieutenant Governor, Sir William Muir, appreciated the efforts of the Institute which were directed to the promotion of schools for girls.[15] He emphasised that this was a work of great importance, because mothers themselves educated, are in the best possible position to impart education to their children for, he thought, no teaching could be so useful and valuable as that which the mother imparts to her children. This was looked upon by him as the best beginning and foundation of all other learning, which would be entirely lost to the children, if the women remained uneducated. Similar speeches and addresses by the British officials given from different kinds of forums during this time are on record. They did seem to mould, to a certain extent, the public opinion in favour of female education. Even the group led by Syed Ahmad Khan publishing the *Aligarh Institute Gazette*, were somewhat influenced by this propaganda in favour of female education. In a write-up on 'Female Education-A National Necessity', in the *Aligarh Institute Gazette* 1869, it is asserted that it would be foolish not to take advantage of the helping hand extended by the Government towards female education, especially when the aid was not 'officiously' and 'gratuitously' offered, but was being offered in answer to the evident need and general desire of the people.[16] This shows that at this time quite influential groups were persuaded to give up their apathy towards female education and they were not openly hostile to the Government's policy of assistance towards that cause. Sir John Lawrence, the Viceroy, also tried to convince these sections by stating that 'of all the measures affecting the permanent good of the higher classes of the natives of India, female education was the most important' and went forward in authorizing grants for that purpose. In 1864, he authorized a grant of 800 pounds in the Punjab, increased in 1865 by another 1000 pounds.[17]

The Government policy regarding the education of girls was that of encouragement by relaxing the rules pertaining to girls' schools. The system of grants-in-aid inaugurated by Woods Dispatch was used to encourage 'native' efforts in this field. Grants-in-aid rules required that the school applying for support be under adequate local management, that local support and fees account for at least half of the expenses of the school, and that a good standard of education be imparted. Periodic Government inspection would ensure that the above conditions were met. In the case of girls' schools, all or any of these conditions might not be applied. For example, in the case of a missionary school applying for a grant there was no question of local management. Hence the fact that a number of girls attended the school more or less regularly might be taken as evidence of adequate local support. It was also difficult for girls' schools to attract fees paying students. Thus this requirement was also dropped for girls' schools and sometimes students were actually paid a small sum per day for attending school, or given free food and clothing.[18] All this meant the relaxation of the requirement that a substantial portion of the school's expenses be met locally.

Finally, the question of inspection to ensure an adequate standard of education was problematic, for government educational inspectors were men, and the parents of girls were against their daughters being examined by male inspectors.[19] By the 1880s government inspectresses were beginning to be appointed.[20]

These concessions resulted in an increase in the number of girls' schools and the number of girls being taught, but it also meant that the quality of education the girls were receiving was often very poor or non-existent.[21]

The problems of finding teachers and of ensuring a certain standard of instruction were only two of the obstacles encountered by the government. A third, affecting Muslim girls particularly, was the custom of purdah. Up to the age of about 10, little girls were not secluded and they could therefore go out to school or even be taught with little boys. Thereafter they needed to go to a different school, or were simply withdrawn from school altogether. This situation was further aggravated by the custom of early marriage. Both Hindu and Muslim girls were married at 10 or12, after which they seldom returned to school unless their husbands or fathers-in-law approved.[22]

After the Educational Durbar held at Lahore in February 1862 under the Presidentship of Sir Robert Montgomery, the Lt Governor of Punjab, there was a substantial increase in the number of girls' schools in the Punjab.[23] The increase in the number of schools amounted to about one thousand, with twenty thousand on the rolls.[24] But these schools were almost entirely devoted to elementary religious instruction.[25] Of these, two-thirds were classed as aided schools, being more under the patronage of 'Native' committees, and to some extent being maintained by them. The girls attending these schools were Hindus and Muslims in nearly equal proportion, though the Government schools contained a large majority of Muslim girls, and the aided schools more Hindu girls.[26] From 1865-1872, there was a steady decrease in the number of girls' schools and of the pupils in attendance, at first owing to the withdrawal of a Government grant of Rs.10,000 and afterwards by the continual elimination of unsatisfactory schools.[27]

Statistics for the attendance of Muslim girls in schools are not available for other provinces, probably because the number of school-going Muslim girls in these provinces was negligible. The fact that the Muslim girls in the Punjab region attended schools in nearly equal numbers to that of Hindu girls seems to show that the Muslims of the Punjab region, as compared to other provinces, were more responsive in their attitude towards female education. This is also borne by the statistics collected by the Muhammadan Educational Conference. The statistics collected and printed in the proceedings of the Muhammadan Educational Conference mainly relate to the Punjab. Significantly enough, in the Punjab, the Muslim girls not only attended schools meant for themselves exclusively, but also attended schools together with girls of other religions. For example, in Lahore and Amritsar, Muslim girls in large numbers attended municipal schools as well as schools run by the Shiksha Sabha.[28] But the families who sent their girls to schools did not belong to the '*ashraf*. The reasons given in the Proceedings of the Muhammadan Educational Conference for the reluctance of the *ashraf* to send their girls to these schools was that they did not approve of their daughters mixing with girls coming from 'poor' (*garib*) families and also because no instruction in religion was imparted.[29]

Outside the Punjab, the only other region about which we get some information in the Proceedings of the Muhammadan Educational Conference indicating growing interest among sections of Muslims in female education was the Central Provinces. A report appearing in the Proceedings of the Muhammadan Educational Conference of 1886 goes to indicate that there existed government as well as missionary schools in Jabalpur which were also attended by Muslim girls though their number could not be ascertained.

As a result of all these constraints, the government's encouragement of female education was at best limited. The missionary societies, on the other hand, braved the cultural resistance and instituted *zenana* teaching. In this work, women missionaries could do, what even elderly male teachers could not; go into the *zenana* and teach women.

According to a witness before the Education Commission of 1882, most of the schools returned as 'government schools' in the Director's Reports owed their prosperity and, in some cases their origin, to the active interest taken in them by English ladies. There were, besides, working in the Punjab, more than twelve missionary and benevolent societies, six of these solely intended for female education and *zenana* work. All these societies had girls' schools and *zenana* classes (i.e. classes held inside the female apartments of Indian families) under them.[30] Initially, girls' schools under the auspices of missions were for the children of the Christian converts only. But later, the missionaries set up institutions for the education of non-Christian girls also, particularly in Bengal, Bombay and Madras.[31]The ladies engaged in *zenana* classes taught the children to read and write, and also to do needlework.

There was, however, the ever present apprehension of conversions in these schools.[32] Nearly all the non-Christian witnesses in their answer to the Education Commission of 1882, were of the opinion that the primary motive of these missionaries was proselytism. Unlike the Europeans, especially the missionary ladies, who believed that they were exercising 'a most wholesome moral and civilizing influence on their minds' through their efforts at female education, the non-Christian witnesses before the Commission thought otherwise. They agreed that some benefits were accruing to them through *zenana* teaching, but that on the whole the missionary ladies did not have much of a share in female education for they were found only in cities and towns. Also, people availed of their services only sparingly. The orthodox families did not allow them access into their houses for they thought they would be polluted by contact.[33] Another obstacle confronting these ladies, it was believed, was the ignorance on their part, of the vernacular of the Province. In the Urdu speaking areas *zenana* teaching might have been comparatively easier; for it seems the missionary ladies in the Punjab all knew Urdu and English.[34]

The system of teaching modern subjects through female instructors inside the homes of the local people was, however, carried on almost entirely by the missionary societies. According to one of the witnesses[35] before the Commission, 'more than 30 European ladies are engaged in carrying on female education in the Punjab, either by superintending boarding and day schools or by *zenana* teaching. Secular as well as religious instruction is given by these ladies and their assistants in hundreds of houses to 'Native' gentleman's wives and daughters, who being *purdah-nasheen*, could not attend schools.'

In the Punjab, of the aided girls' schools, one middle school and three primary schools in which English was taught, and eighty-two vernacular primary schools, were managed by the missionary ladies. The number of girls' schools under the missionary ladies had increased from thirty-six in 1871 to fifty-six in 1876, and eighty-six in 1882.[36]

In 1882, there were two agencies for *zenana* instruction in the Central Provinces. One was that of the Free Church of Scotland at Nagpur and the other was that of the Church of England Mission at Jabalpur.[37] As in the Punjab, at these places as well, the missionary ladies went to the *zenana* apartments to teach. Though the chief aim of the *zenana* mission teachers was propagation of Christianity, they also taught most of the *zenana* pupils arithmetic, geography, grammar, reading and writing. These missions also had four girls' schools attended by seventy-five students. Sixty-six girls and adults were taught in the *zenana*. Together, there were thus one hundred and forty one pupils, of whom two were Christians, one hundred and twenty-five Hindus and fourteen Muslims.[38] As the work of these missionary agencies was confined to Nagpur and Jabalpur, the total number of girls benefitted by their efforts was rather small.[39]

United Provinces lagged behind in the field of education. Many of its schools established by the colonial administration under the Charles Wood Dispatch Act, 1854, as well as schools of missionaries, were demolished in the upsurge of 1857.[40]

But after a gap, in the post-1857 period, the British administration again made some attempts to promote women's education in the province. The British knew that the local population was averse to female education. People did not send their daughters to schools, especially to those schools where there were male teachers. Therefore they opened *zenana* schools (Girls schools where all teachers were females). One of the important aims of these schools was to produce a class of trained female teachers who could further contribute in promoting women's education. Christian missionaries also established *zenana* schools in some parts of the province.[41] However, it must be said that the local population generally did not welcome the missionary schools, as they feared these schools would induce people to convert to Christianity.[42]

The British Administration established a normal *zenana* school at Lucknow in 1868.[43] The school primarily aimed at producing trained female teachers for girls of 'natives'.[44] A European lady was appointed to supervise the school. Initially 20 students were enrolled in the school in 1868, but their number declined to seven in 1881 and again increased to 19 in 1891. All the students belonged to the Muslim community. Firdous Azmat Siddiqui in her study 'Muslim Women's Education in the United Provinces: A Case Study of Allahabad University' is of the opinion that there was a positive response by the Muslims to the *zenana* school established by the British government.

Another *zenana* school was established at Faizabad during this period. The school progressed well because of the individual effort of Miss Reuthor who had a good knowledge of Urdu.[45]

Archival sources of the province show that many *zenana* schools were established in the province after 1870. There was a *zenana* school in the town of Nawabganj, district Pratapgarh, which was managed by the Deputy Inspector of Schools, Mufti Mohammad Husain. The school had an enrollment of 13 students in 1878.[46]

A school for widows was opened by Munshi Zakaullah in Bulandshahar during that period.[47]

About 100 *zenana* schools were opened by 1875, of which 16 were aided schools, 81 were under government control, and 3 were privately controlled.[48]

Literacy level of Muslim women in the United Provinces was not uniform. It differed from region to region and within a region from one class to another. In comparison to the central and eastern parts of the province, Muslims were numerically more in the western parts of the province. Many of them were landlords or belonged to the professional classes. Economically they were more advanced than the Muslims of the central and eastern parts. Despite their economic prosperity, however, the literacy level of Muslim women was low in the western parts of the province. Indeed, poor economic condition of Muslims in the central and eastern regions of the province motivated them for acquiring modern education in order to elevate their socio-economic status. Missionary schools had more appeal for them than for the Muslims of the western regions. Hence the literacy level of Muslim women in the central and eastern regions of the province was more than their counter-parts in the western regions.[49]

In 1885, the establishment of the Lady Dufferin Fund had cleared the way for women to acquire medical education. Though there were no women in this province considered eligible to get admission for an MBBS degree, there were many women of both communities who took the 2 year or 3 year diploma courses for 'midwife', 'nurse', 'hospital assistant' and '*da'i*' at the Agra Medical College and other colleges. In 1889, there were 8 Muslim women out of 19 who were enrolled in the diploma course. It is also important to note that there were no women who belonged to upper classes/castes of Hindus or to the Muslim '*ashraf*' class.[50]

The *zenana* teaching started by the missionaries was mainly patronised by the Muslim '*ashraf*' families, who did not send their girls to the government schools or the mission schools, though some of these families were not totally averse to sending their daughters to the schools established by the Anjuman-e-Islamia, a private organization.

The earliest voluntary instance of private enterprise among Muslims in the field of female education was among the Muslims of Bangalore. As early as 1867 a school was established specifically for Muslim girls in Bangalore and it seems that this school was the only one of its kind till then to be established by the Muslims. The schools numbered some eighty pupils.[51]

In general it was in the Punjab that the earliest voluntary efforts by the Muslims to establish girls' schools were registered. In making these efforts the Muslims were motivated mainly by a desire to counter the influence of the missionaries who were believed to be trying to propagate their religion under the cover of educational efforts. In the Punjab, around 1884, the Muslims started establishing local organizations called Anjuman-i-Islamia to provide 'proper' education for Muslim girls and boys. The Lahore Anjuman-i-Islamia was established in 1884.A similar organization with the designation Anjuman-i-Himayat-Islam came into existence in Amritsar. This organization too is credited for making a contribution, though on a limited scale, towards the education of Muslim girls. The Lahore Anjuman-i-Islamia is reported to have established schools on the traditional pattern for the education of Muslim girls belonging to the *ashraf* families. The funds for running these schools were raised by 'respectable' and the rich Muslim families of the Punjab.[52] Instructions imparted in these schools were mainly religious in character, so as to keep the girls "protected from the influence of other religions."[53]In a speech at the Muhammadan Educational Congress in 1888, Sheikh Khairuddin speaks of no less than twelve schools of this kind in the Punjab with more than three hundred girls on the rolls.[54]

There exists evidence suggesting that an organization calling itself Anjuman-i-Islamia also came into existence at Jabalpur sometime between 1882 and 1886.The rough idea about the time this organization came into existence at Jabalpur can be deduced from the fact that, while in the testimony tendered before the Education Commission of 1882, there is no mention of this organization, in the report presented to the Muhammadan Educational Congress of 1886, it is referred to as an established body. In this school established by the Anjuman-i-Islamia in Jabalpur, two lady teachers were employed and seventy girls studied the Quran besides learning arithmetic, sewing and needlework.[55]

The girls observed purdah and *dolis* were arranged for them to take them to and from the schools. Girls above the age of eleven were not admitted in the schools, and those of them already admitted were withdrawn without the completion of their study as soon as they reached the age of eleven.[56]

It is significant that the voluntary Muslim effort for establishing girls' schools in the Punjab and certain parts of Central Provinces became discernible almost simultaneously. Even the name of the private organizations formed in the two regions for this purpose is identical, namely Anjuman-i-Islamia. This goes to suggest that the efforts in these places had a common inspiration. The situation in which the Anjuman-i-Islamia emerged had many similarities. In Jabalpur, as in Lahore, the missionaries were very active in imparting female education and had considerable impact on the Muslim population also. At both places, the Christian missionaries were looked upon with suspicion, and these voluntary organizations were formed with an aim to counter the efforts of the Christian missionaries at conversion. This in turn leads to the inference that Muslim private effort for establishing schools for girls during this period was mainly motivated by their anxiety to counter the proselytizing activities of the Christian missions. Such efforts surfaced at a very early stage precisely in those regions where Christian missionaries were particularly active among the Muslims.

Thus it can be seen that in the 19th and early 20th century, among the Muslims, apparently, female education was not considered an important prerequisite for the overall progress of the community. Secular education was to have only a minimal place in the curricula. It was only with the rise of the Aligarh Movement that some sort of concrete efforts were directed towards Muslim women's education.

References

1. Nurullah and Naik (1951), p. 24.
2. *Selections from Educational Records*, Part II, 1840-1859, ed. J.A. Richey, C.I.E., p.32, published for the National Archives of India by the Manager of Publications, Government of India, 1965.
3. Ibid.
4. Ibid.
5. Ibid, pp. 59-60.
6. Ibid.
7. Ibid, p. 388.
8. *Talism*, Lucknow, 24th April 1857, No.4, Vol. I. .
9. Education Dispatch No.4 dated 7th April 1859, from the Secretary of State of India, para 47 (National Archives of India).
10. Report of the Director of Public Instruction (NWP) 1870-71,Vol. II. Appendix 'E', Part 'C' as quoted in Francis Robinson, *Separatism among Indian Muslims 1860-1923*, Delhi, 1975, p.87.
11. *The Aligarh Institute Gazette*, Jan 31st 1868, No. 5, Vol. III.
12. Ibid.
13. Extract from G.O. No. 616 dated 10th Oct.1868 from the officiating Secretary, Government of India, to the Secretary, Government of N. W. P., with reference to the wording of G.O. No.2583 dated 20th July

1867 of the Government of India, published in the *Aligarh Institute Gazette* 1869, No.4, Vol. IV.

14. Report of the Director of Public Instruction (N.W.P) 1870-71, Vol. II. Appendix E. Part C, as quoted in Francis Robinson *Separatism Among Indian_Muslims*, p.87.
15. *Aligarh Institute Gazette* 1869, No.3. Vol. IV. Speech by the Lt. Governor, Sir William Muir, K.S.C.I., to the Shahjahanpore Institute, 19th December 1868.
16. *Aligarh Institute Gazette* 1869, No. 48, Vol. IV, 'Female Education-A National Necessity'.
17. *Aligarh Institute Gazette* 1875, No. 5, Vol. X.
18. Appendix to the Education Commission Report (Punjab) 1884, Chapter XX, p.60.
19. (i) Education Commission Report 1884, pp. 542-547; (ii) Evidence of Mrs. Mary Chatterjee before the Education Commission 1882, (Punjab), p.175.
20. Education Commission Report 1884, pp. 542-547.
21. (i) Education Commission Report,_1884, pp. 542-547; (ii) Evidence of Dr. G.V. Lietner. L.L.D., before the Education Commission 1882, p.380.
22. Note by E.C. Bayley, Secretary, Government of India, dated 22nd June 1867, Home Education Consultation Nos. 8-10, dated August 1867, p.60.
23. Appendix to the Education Commission Report, (Punjab) 1884, Chapter V, p.10.
24. Ibid.
25. Appendix to the Education Commission Report, (Punjab) 1884, Chapter XX, p.60.
26. Ibid.
27. Ibid.
28. Muhammadan Educational Congress, 1888, p.18.
29. Ibid.
30. Evidence of Mrs. Mary Chatterjee before the Education Commission 1882, (Punjab), p.175.

31. Selections from Educational Records, Part II, (1840-1859), p.34.
32. P. Thomas, *Indian Women through the Ages*, Bombay, 1964, p. 311.
33. Evidence of the Lahore Arya Samaj before the Education Commission, 1882 (Punjab), p.478.
34. Ibid.
35. Appendix to the Education Commission Report, (Punjab) 1884, Chapter XX, p.60.
36. Ibid.
37. Appendix to the Education Commission Report, (Central Provinces) 1884, p.76.
38. Ibid.
39. Evidence of Mr. Ambica Charan Banerji before the Education Commission, 1882, (Central Provinces), p.163.
40. Siddiqui, Firdous Azmat, 'Muslim Women's Education in the United Provinces: A Case Study of Allahabad University', AMU 2007. p. 215.
41. *The Development of Women's Education in India*, ed. Sabyasachi Bhattacharya, Joseph Bara, Chinna Rao Yagati, Sankhdher, 2001, Kanishka Publishers, Distributors, New Delhi.
42. *The Aligarh Institute Gazette*, 13th March 1894. Article by Haji Mohd. Ismail Khan.
43. Home: Education, 31 Oct. 1868, File Nos. 3-4. Siddiqui, Firdous Azmat, op. cit., p. 215.
44. Ibid.
45. Ibid, 3rd September 1868.
46. *Gazetteer of the Province of Oudh*, Vol. III, N-Z, Allahabad, NWP and Oudh. Government Press, 1878, p. 136 as quoted in Siddiqui, Firdous Azmat op. cit., p. 216.
47. *Aligarh Magazine, Khawateen* Number, 2001, Aligarh Muslim University, Aligarh, p. 33.
48. *The Development of Women's Education in India*, ed. Sabyasachi Bhattacharya et. al.
49. Census Report of India NWP of Agra and Oudh, 1921, ed. 1902, Allahabad, p.154 as quoted in Siddiqui, Firdous Azmat op. cit., p. 219.
50. Ibid., p. 220.

51. *Aligarh Institute Gazette*, 1887, No. 40, Vol. II. 'Mohammadan Female Education', extract from 'Friday Review'.
52. Muhammadan Educational Congress, 1888. Speech of Sheikh Khair-uddin, p.110.
53. Muhammadan Educational Congress, 1889, p.60.
54. Muhammadan Educational Congress, 1888. Speech of Sheikh Khair-uddin, p.110.
55. Muhammadan Educational Congress, 1886, p.11.
56. Ibid.

CHAPTER III

Aligarh Movement and Muslim Women's Education, 1875-1902

Northern India was passing through a phase of reforms. Muslim reformers too were now zealously advocating female education. Spread of female education, according to them would help in making women better house managers, competent mothers and also in becoming rational and less vulnerable to superstitions. That purdah is not to be a hindrance in the spread of education among Muslim females was time and again reiterated by Syed Mumtaz Ali, Nazir Ahmad, and the Nawab of Bhopal, Begum Sultan Jahan. Maulana Ashraf Ali Thanwi in *Bihishti Zewar*, Nazir Ahmad in *Mirat-ul-Urus* and Altaf Hussain Hali in *Majalis-un-Nisa* strongly advocated female education and the benefits accruing thereof.

The ideal form of education was a topic much discussed by the reformers. The progressive Urdu newspapers were also supporting female education. The first women's Urdu magazine *Akhbar-un-Nisa* of Syed Ahmad Dehelvi supported female education.[1]

A majority of these Muslim intellectuals were in favour of imparting education to women that was limited to religion, knowledge of how to read and write, elementary mathematics and the basics of household management.

Sir Syed Ahmad Khan through his papers *Tahzib-ul-Akhlaq* and *Aligarh Institute Gazette* also supported female education in the initial years. "I have lamented the custom by which the females of India are left in ignorance, and have urged upon you the necessity, if you would really seek to elevate the social position of the people, of educating your girls."[2] But we will see the contradictions in his viewpoints as he became more involved with the education of Muslims.

Nazir Ahmad Khan, while talking about the benefits of female education, mentions that education would help women perform their duties sincerely and make them more virtuous, efficient and competent. He condemned the popular notion that education would make women irresponsible. He appealed to the opponents of female education to change their attitude regarding education.[3]

Hali's *Majalis un-Nisa* (Assemblies of Women) is in the form of conversations among middle-class Muslim women of Delhi, conversations which include long narrative passages describing women's daily life, their education and training in household management, child-rearing practices, customs and beliefs. Its message: Women should be educated because they are the real managers of the household, the focus of family life, responsible for the early training of the children. *Majalis* was thus a plea for reform, and reflected not only actual conditions at the time, but also Hali's ideas of how things should be. It is a work of social history reflecting the language, home life, beliefs, and practices of urban middle-class Muslims in the mid to late nineteenth century. It is an eloquent and engaging plea for women's education and greater recognition of women's rights within their traditional family roles. Col. Holroyd recommended *Majalis* for a literary prize, and Lord Northbrooke, the Viceroy, awarded Hali 400 rupees for the work. *Majalis* was adopted as a textbook for girls' schools in the Punjab and United Provinces for decades thereafter. It is significant that Hali was considerably more advanced in his thinking on women's education than was Sir Syed Ahmed Khan, who in the mid-1870s was engaged in founding Aligarh College. In his testimony before the Indian Education Commission of 1882, Sir Syed maintained that a little education was enough for women. Until more Muslim men received a sound education, Muslim women would have to wait: "The present state of education among Muhammadan females is, in my opinion, enough for domestic happiness." Hali, on the other hand, not only wrote *Majalis*, but also started a couple of schools for girls in his home town of Panipat, run by the women of his family.

Hali's poem in praise of Muslim women, *Chup ki Dad*, was written at the request of Sheikh Abdullah, a young Aligarh lawyer, a graduate of Sir Syed's college, and Secretary of the Women's Education Section of the Muhammadan Educational Conference. The poem was first published in Sheikh Abdullah's reformist Urdu journal for women, *Khatoon*, in December 1905. In it, Hali reiterates many of the ideas he had originally espoused in *Majalis*: Women are the true strength of the family and the community, but lamentably many of them are kept in ignorance; thus women's education is vital for the regeneration of the Muslim community. The following year, 1906, Sheikh Abdullah and his wife founded the Aligarh Girls' School in the face of great opposition, but with the patronage of Nawab Sultan Jahan Begam, the ruler of Bhopal, whose monetary aid is commemorated in the closing lines of the poem. Both Hali and Sheikh Abdullah had good reason to acknowledge the importance of patronage in accomplishing their goals. Apart from the schools for girls he established, he also raised funds to found a public library in Panipat and had visions of starting a Muslim High School in the town, a project brought to fruition after his death by his son, Khwaja Sajjad Husain. He died on December 31, 1914.[4]

Altaf Hussain Hali's *Majlis-un-Nisa* has argued for female education. Hali believed that for the upliftment of the country, the awakening of

> the neglected half of the human race, that is the women of the country, is a must. The main character of the novel, Aatuji is an educated and accomplished lady who firmly believes that the spread of education among women will help in removing the widespread superstitions and evil customs among them. She is also of the opinion that the first step in a child's education begins in his or her mother's lap. 'It is the mother who initially moulds her child's character.[5]
>
> Atauji believes that keeping our daughters ignorant is against the will of God. On the day of justice, he will definitely question the guilty parents for the discrimination made by them in the arrangements of their sons and daughters. God has not created daughters to lead miserable lives like cats and dogs. They are supposed to have their own identities and also to have capabilities to realize the true nature of their own souls and that of God. They are also meant to utilize their brains and do justice to their birth as a human being.[6]

Syed Mumtaz Ali, the famous educationist of Lahore and editor of the magazine *Tahzib-un-Niswan* was a staunch supporter of female education and believed that progress could not be achieved without the spread of female education. Mumtaz Ali says that those who feel that a rudimentary knowledge of prayers, cooking, sewing, taking care of children is enough for girls, and that further education would make the girl disobedient, are arguing baselessly. He further argues that it is not possible to find out whether further education would prove to be dangerous unless one gives it a chance. The danger comes from depriving women of the full moral and mental development of their faculties rather than from giving women an education. A mere recital of prayers does not equip women to be aware of their moral rights and duties. Women also should have knowledge of bringing up children, running a home and be a suitable companion to their husband. For all this they need more than just a rudimentary education. The whole society would suffer if an inadequately educated woman does not know how to raise her children. If she does not provide good company, her husband may go astray and seek such company elsewhere, thus breaking the family. "For the survival of the Muslim family and of

Muslim civilization as a whole, therefore, the education of women to their fullest potential is necessary."[7]

The magazine *Ismat* published from Delhi by Rashidul Khairi strongly supported female education. Articles appearing in the magazine in support of female education time and again show that it played an important role in formulating public support for the cause.[8]

Through Anjuman-i-Khawatin-i-Islam, in the Punjab, the contribution of people like Shah Din and his niece Begum Jahanara Shahnawaz for the cause of female education became obvious. Through her book *Tahzib-un-Niswan wa Tarbiyat-al-Insan* she talked of religious education together with sufficient knowledge of domestic science.[9]

In his article '*Haq aur Farz*' Nawab Mohsinul Mulk argued that the spread of female education is an essential prerequisite for a nation's progress. Efforts made for the growth and development of a nation would prove to be futile without the spread of female education.[10]

An interesting piece of poetry published in *Madina*, in 1913, throws light on how beneficial effects of education for women were perceived at the time. Education would not only rid them (the women) of all superstitions, injustices and ignorance, but also make them cultured and provide them with self-respect. It would help them in their own progress and in guiding the future generations to become perfect human beings

Gar mard hamein likhne parhne ki raza denge,
Ham naam jihalat ka, duniya se mita denge,
Farmane Khuda, apni ankhon se jo dekhenge,
Taamil ki khatir phir ankhon ko bicha denge,
Shauhar ki itaat mein, Allah kit aid mein,
Ham dil ko laga denge, ham jaan ko laga denge,
Taalim ki bijli ka, jab dil pe asar hoga,

Naadani ke khirman ko, ham aag laga denge,
Har waham parasti ko, har beedate hasti ko,
Sukhe hue patton ki, surat se ura denge,
Taalim bana degi, akhlaq ko jab ala,
Ham oonche tarakki par, khud ja ke dikha denge,
Tehzib hamein haasil,taalim se jab hgi,
Naslon ko tumhari ham,insane bana denge[11]

Those among the Muslims advocating women's education did not approve of higher education for them, but wanted to limit their education to the boundaries of domesticity, so that they become better managers of their homes, better wives, better mothers and better persons. These ideas are reminiscent of similar arguments for women's education in other parts of the country. These reformers were not any more backward than those who argued for education for Hindu women. As elsewhere, the thought of education as a means of empowerment or economic independence did not ever cross their minds. To augment their household income, Sir Syed Ahmad Khan, Altaf Hussain Hali, Nazir Ahmad and the Begum of Bhopal suggested various handicrafts.

Female education had to be spread without annoying the supporters of the custom of purdah, a religiously sanctioned custom for Muslim women. They had to tread the path of female education very cautiously.

Akbar Allahabadi, the great satirical poet, was not against the spread of female education. However, he did not approve of their becoming 'socialites' but instead wanted them to become 'good housewives'.

Taalim Larkiyon ki, lazim to hai magar,
Khatun-i-khana ho, who sabha ki pari na ho

In another piece of satire, he says that an educated daughter may dance in her own marriage procession.[12]

Taalim –i-dakhtaran se yeh ummid hai zaroor,
Nache khushi se dulhan khud apni barat mein

Imparting modern education to women and granting freedom to them was regarded against the teachings of Islam. In *Nayar-i-Azam*, Moradabad, it is said that granting freedom to women of this enslaved country will be disastrous to the Muslim community.[13]

The Begum of Bhopal, Nawab Sultan Jahan Begum, in her speech at Madarsa-i-Sultania regards the custom of purdah as having religious sanction, and therefore mandatory for every Muslim woman. She suggests various ways to impart education to purdah-observing women, and at the same time warns the supporters of female education against revolt with regard to the custom of purdah, as society would never approve of it and it would only hamper their efforts.[14]

Syed Karamat Hussain, the great educationist of Lucknow, did not find any fault in economic independence of women by pursuing knowledge and skill in any craft. In 1899 at the Graduate Association he proposed to provide technical education to the purdah observing Muslim girls.[15]

Thus we see that a conducive atmosphere was being created for the rise and spread of Muslim female education, which in turn gave rise to fierce debates as to the content of the curriculum and the method of education to be adopted, especially for Muslim girls.

Syed Ahmad Khan on Muslim Female Education

The one person whose ideas and views on Muslim female education had a great impact and were of immense importance to the lives of Muslim men and women in nineteenth century India was Sir Syed Ahmad Khan.

Sir Syed Ahmad Khan (1817-1898), an intellectual, a jurist, a reformer, a visionary, a redeemer of the Muslim community in India from the post 1857 trauma and the founder of the Mohammedan Anglo Oriental College in 1875, which later became Aligarh Muslim University, at Aligarh, Uttar Pradesh, India, belonged to one of the few '*ashraf*' families of Delhi where education was held in high esteem. Syed Ahmad Khan told his fellow Muslims that modern education and learning were the means through which one could empower the Self.[16]

Syed Ahmed Khan galvanized Indian Muslims to raise money for the foundation of a school for boys at Aligarh by warning them: "If the Muslims do not take to the system of education introduced by the English they will not only remain a backward community, but will sink lower until there will be no hope of recovery left to them…how we can remain true Muslims or serve Islam if we sink into ignorance?"[17]

To Syed Ahmad Khan and to the majority of his addressees, Muslims meant only 'male' Muslims and the community was restricted only to the 'male' community. In fact, he characterised the new education that he encouraged his fellow men to acquire as "unsuited to the domestic and social requirements of the Muslim community."[18] Indeed education was considered dangerous for women.[19]

He was against the government-sponsored system of education for Muslim girls and opposed modern education and schools for Muslim women. He strongly advised Muslim women to adhere to the traditional system of education that alone would help them in their moral and material well-being. Once educated, Muslim men, he felt, would, in turn educate their female relatives. Suitable curricula for girls would be "domestic crafts, respect for their elders, affection for the husband, care of the children and understanding of religious tenets." He approved only these aspects of education for Muslim women and expressed his disgust for anything beyond that.[20]

C.E. Trevalyan in his reply to questions asked before the Parliamentary Committee in London in 1853 as to the causes for the 'hostility to female education as exists in the Hindu mind' (any reference to the Hindu women is equally applicable to Muslim women as well) was convinced enough to reply that they perceived it thus: 'in order to keep the women in subjection, it is necessary to keep them ignorant.'[21]

Sir Syed Ahmad Khan during the early years of his career, especially in the late 1860s and 1870s, had appeared favourably inclined towards Muslim female education. In the sixties, the *Aligarh Institute Gazette*, influenced to a great extent by Syed Ahmad Khan, published articles on government policy encouraging female education, hailing its successful implementation in different places. From this one can infer that initially Syed Ahmad Khan was not totally opposed to women's education or the establishment of schools for them. In 1867, the establishment a Muslim girls' school in Bangalore solely by indigenous efforts was acclaimed with great pleasure and appreciation in a write-up entitled 'Mohammadan Female Education' that appeared in the *Aligarh Institute Gazette*, Vol. II, of 1867. In this write-up female education was considered to form the 'groundwork of the social, moral and intellectual advancement of a nation,' which could not rise to true greatness so long as its women were allowed to remain in intellectual darkness.[22]

In 1869 and in the subsequent years we find articles in the *Aligarh Institute Gazette* on the importance of female education and its spread as the chief means for the general spread of education.

A letter that Sir Syed Ahmad Khan wrote from London to the Secretary, Scientific Society, Aligarh, in 1869, also gives the same impression. He wrote that he was highly impressed by his landlady's daughter, who when she was ill, took to reading religious books which he thought she would find "too abstruse and uninteresting because of their controversial nature." He goes on to comment, "From these remarks you will see how well bred and intelligent are the women of even the middle classes here. Is it not instructive and worthy of admiration that a woman on her sick bed would try to amuse herself and beguile her time by such a cheerful occupation as that? Have you ever heard or seen any raja or chief, noble or gentleman in India (not to speak of women) resorting to so judicious and wholesome a means of amusement in their sickness? Do the Indians possess such a literary taste and love for knowledge?"[23]

He was also appreciative of the progress of Muslim women's education which he had observed when he passed through Turkey and Egypt.[24]

However, there are indications of a reversal in Syed Ahmed Khan's thinking with respect to female education from 1880 onwards. Henceforth, he started opposing any step taken by the government for education of Muslim women. An early instance of such an attitude can be found in his answers to the questions put to him by the Education Commission of 1882.[25]

In his answers he emphasizes that the general idea held that "Mohammadan ladies of respectable families are ignorant" is wrong. In fact he claimed that a sort of indigenous education of a moderate degree prevailed among them and they studied religious and moral books in Urdu and Persian and in some instances in Arabic as well. He mentions some instances of ladies of his own family who could read, speak and understand Arabic fairly well, could read and teach Persian books on morality, and could write letters in Persian and compose verses in their own language. This he felt was not a new or a rare thing as he himself had received his early training in morals and 'other instructive lessons' from his mother. He goes on to say that the well to do and the 'respectable' among the Muslim families employ female tutors (*ustanis* or *mullanis*) to get their girls instructed in the Quran and in elementary theological books in the Urdu language. Sometimes, the fathers or the brothers impart instructions to them in Persian and English, sufficient for the purpose of writing telegraphic messages. In spite of all this, he admits "that the general state of female education among Muslims is far from satisfactory." And his reply to the question whether Government could take any step towards the education of Muslim girls was that it was not possible for Government to adopt any practical measure by which the 'respectable Mohammadans' may be induced to send their daughters to Government schools for education. Nor, he claimed, could Government bring into existence a school on which the parents and guardians of girls may place perfect reliance. The Muslims, he pointed out, could not be blamed for this disinclination towards Government schools considering "the State in which these are in the country." He emphasized again that the efforts made till then by the Government to provide education to the Muslim girls had all been in vain and had completely failed to produce any effect whatever upon the respectable Muslim families. Nor had the lower classes derived any benefit from them. Any endeavour on the part of the Government to introduce female education among Muslims would, under the social circumstances then prevailing, prove a complete failure and would probably produce mischievous results and be a waste of money and energy.[26]

Syed Ahmed Khan held that those who thought that women should be 'educated and civilized' then were greatly mistaken. According to him, no satisfactory education could be provided for Muslim women until a large number of Muslim men received a sound education. The state of education among the Muslim women was, in his opinion, enough for domestic happiness, considering the prevalent social and economic conditions of the Muslims in India. He thought that the government should concentrate its efforts on the education and enlightenment of Muslim boys, and when a generation of Muslim men became well educated and enlightened, the circumstances would necessarily have a powerful though indirect effect on the enlightenment of Muslim women "for enlightened fathers, brothers and husbands, would naturally be most anxious to educate their female relations."[27]

An exposition of such an attitude in a much more explicit language is again found in his reply to an Address presented to him in 1884 in Gurdaspur on behalf of the women of Punjab.[28] In his reply he said that he was not indifferent towards the education of women of his community and wholeheartedly desired their educational advancement. But he was opposed to modern education for them, and advised women to adhere to the traditional system of education that alone would help them in their moral and material well-being, and protect them from difficulties. He claimed that efforts at educating the Muslim boys was in fact an effort for the well being of both boys and girls, as the condition of women would improve automatically in consequence of the improved condition of men.[29]

He did not want girls to acquire the habit of reading "useless (*Na Mufied, Na Mubarak*) modern books instead of reading holy and pure books which were read by their grandmothers. The men who are the bread winners of the families, in response to the need of the changing world, had to acquire new skills or learn a new language." In other words, according to him, it was because of economic necessity that it was essential for the boys to imbibe modern education which would enable them to get government jobs. But these changes had nothing to do with girls. So the old and traditional system of education was still relevant for them. Syed Ahmad Khan admitted that the equal rights that were given by God to women had been abrogated by virtue of the illiteracy and ignorance of men. To get back those rights, the only way was to educate boys. When men are educated, women's rights would automatically be restored to them.

Syed Ahmad Khan seems inconsistent in his outlook on education. In the first place he takes modern education to be necessary for the boys because of economic necessity. On the other hand he also considers it a virtue, for he says that women will be given back their rights by men once they are educated; education taken to mean obviously 'modern' education. So for the time being the education of Muslim women, as most Muslim men agreed, had to take place within the home.

Syed Ahmad Khan had cited the government's intention to force girls to attend schools and give up purdah as one of the causes of the revolt of 1857. Articles in the *Aligarh Institute Gazette* warned reformers not to "set down to prejudice and folly all the restraints and regulations which the wisdom of their ancestors had provided for the security of the honour of their families." He also added: "We wish our women to be educated. But if education means letting them loose to mix with whom they please; if it means that as they increase in learning, they shall deteriorate in morals, if it means the loss of our honour and the invasion of the privacy of our homes – we prefer our honour to the education of our women, even though we may be called obstinate, prejudiced and wrong headed."[30]

Despite such negative views held by Syed Ahmed Khan on women's education, with the passage of time, there emerged a distinct tendency within the Aligarh Movement favouring the spread of education among Muslim women. This tendency became particularly manifest from 1888 onwards. At the Third Annual Conference of the Mohammadan Educational Conference held in Lahore in 1888, a resolution was passed to the effect that "The Mohammadan Educational Conference unanimously agrees to the proposal that Muslims should establish schools for the education of Muslim girls. These schools should be in accord with Islam and of the ways of the '*sharif* section of the Muslims." This resolution was particularly opposed by Syed Ahmed Khan, who was strictly opposed to the establishment of schools for women.[31]

In his speech he argued that the teaching of religion and morals to girls at home on traditional lines was sufficient and that teaching of secular subjects like History, Geography, Algebra and Trigonometry to women was useless. It is remarkable that such a resolution was passed despite Syed Ahmad Khan's stiff opposition. From the wordings of the report about this resolution it also appears that support for it was so overwhelming that eventually Syed Ahmed Khan had to acquiesce to the majority view and the resolution was passed unanimously. This, incidentally, goes to indicate the independent mindedness of a majority of persons involved in the Aligarh Movement at that early stage. They did not hesitate in overruling, perhaps under the influence of Theodore Beck, Principal of M.A.O. College, even Syed Ahmed Khan, the undisputed leader of the movement, on such a sensitive issue.[32]

One may further conjecture that, at least partly, this growing climate favouring women's education was a result of Theodore Beck's influence. He had joined M.A.O. college on 1st February 1884 and by 1888 had already become very influential not only in the affairs of the College but also in those of other organizations representing the Aligarh Movement. This may be on account of the great influence that Theodore Beck came to exercise over Syed Ahmad Khan himself. In the model of educational progress that Beck upheld, education of Muslim women was perhaps considered desirable. It may have been partly due to Beck's influence that Syed Ahmad Khan eventually allowed himself to be persuaded to have the above resolution passed unanimously at the Conference. An example of how Beck and other European teachers of the M.A.O. College were instrumental in creating opinion at Aligarh in favour of women's education is a debate that took place in a meeting of the Siddon's Union Club chaired by Beck on 15th November 1884.

The motion over which the debate took place was cleverly worded, "Spread of female education in India is to be desired but by home tuition and not by schools and colleges." It is significant that this motion, which almost echoed Syed Ahmad Khan's views on the issue, was defeated by a narrow margin of three votes.

However, not withstanding Beck's influence and occasional compromises that Syed Ahmed Khan might have had to make on the issue of women's education, his opposition to the idea of Muslim women studying in schools remained strong. In fact towards the end he became even more uncompromising in his attitudes. According to Sheikh Abdullah, the founder of the Women's College at Aligarh, Syed Ahmed Khan even went to the extent of holding that the girls studying in schools and colleges would become immoral.[33] Sheikh Abdullah also quotes Syed Ahmed Khan's sneering retort to one of the students advocating women's education. "Have you yourself come out of Purdah?"

Apparently this view of Syed Ahmed Khan was shared by many of the senior persons involved in the Aligarh Movement. Nazeer Ahmad, for example, is quoted as remarking that the girls after studying in schools will become unmannered and unmanageable (*Hurdangiyan*).[34]

Likewise, when Ghulam-us-Saqlain, a young supporter of women's education, brought up the topic of Muslim girls' education in front of Syed Ahmed Khan, he was made fun of and was asked if he had come out of purdah.[35]

The implication of this 'funny' remark seems to be that only a woman was expected to take interest in female education. It seems strange that Syed Ahmed Khan, known to be a modernist and a social reformer, could hold such conservative views regarding schooling and secular education for girls. In this regard his attitude seems even more conservative and traditional than that of the ulemas of the Deoband school.[36]

> Sir Syed, in his opposition to women's education, developed two basic arguments: first, he believed that education should come first to Muslim men, who in turn would filter it to women in their households. To him, the concept of women getting education first, and men falling behind, would jeopardize gender relationships and thereby life within households would be fractured. His second argument is mainly built against the usefulness of the government-sponsored system of education for girls. This argument was more about the content of education. Was it suitable to the needs of Indian girls and women? This curriculum, from the beginning, suffered from a lacuna: it was a curriculum primarily devised earlier for boys; it was used for girls' schools by merely adding a note about instruction in home-crafts, provided a qualified mistress was available.[37]

It may be presumed that Syed Ahmed Khan's attitude and views regarding female education represented those held by a large section of the Muslim community during the 1880s and 1890s.

As Sheikh Abdullah says, Syed Ahmed Khan's disapproval of Muslim girls' schools and modern education was probably not based on any religious or rational argument, but his adherence to the purdah system lay at its root.[38]

Mohsinul Mulk, writing in 1905, offers an apologia for Syed Ahmed Khan's opposition to female education. He writes that Syed Ahmed Khan's lack of enthusiasm for the spread of modern education among Muslim girls and the establishment of schools for them was probably because he did not want the Muslim community to be more estranged from his own movement than they already were, for, to have spoken of female education at that time would be inviting trouble, as female education was considered to be an evil in itself and his whole movement would have come to a standstill if he had supported it.[39]

This explanation does not seem convincing enough for it was not that Syed Ahmad Khan was just indifferent or only showed lack of enthusiasm towards modern education for Muslim girls. He, in fact, condemned it in strong terms and that is enough evidence to show that towards the last sixteen years of his life he had no sympathy with girls' schools or modern education for girls.

References

1. Jaswal, G.M., 'The Model Curriculum for Women Formulated by the Muslim Intelligentsia of the Pre-Gandhian Era', *Proceedings of the Indian History Congress*, 67th Session, New Delhi 2006-07, p. 768.
2. Graham, G.F.I., *The Life and Works of Syed Ahmad Khan*, p. 237, London 1885.
3. Ahmad, Nazir, *Mirat-ul-Urus* (Hindi Tr. Madan Lal Jain), New Delhi 1982, pp. 18-21.
4. Minault, Gail (trs.), 'Assemblies of Women' and 'Voices of Silence': English translation of Altaf Husain Hali's two works *Majlis-un-Nisa* and *Chup ki Daad*, Delhi: Chanakya Publications, 1986.
5. Malik, Ram, *Hali*, p. 67, New Delhi, 1982 as quoted in Jaswal, G.M., op. cit., pp. 768-9.
6. Ibid.
7. Minault, Gail, 'Sayyid Mumtaz Ali and *Huquq un Niswan* – An Advocate of Women's Rights in the Late Nineteenth Century', *Modern Asian Studies*, Vol. 24, No. I. February 1990.
8. Jaswal, G.M., op. cit., p. 769.
9. Ibid.
10. Mohsinul Mulk, 'Haq aur Farz', *Khatoon*, February, 1905, p. 118.
11. 'Ek Khatun ke Khayalat', *Madina*, 22 January, 1913, p.12 as quoted in Jaswal, G.M., op. cit.
12. Ibid., p. 771.
13. 'Naiyar-i-Azam', 1st May 1908, *Selections from the Vernacular Newspapers*, Vol. 42, p. 428, U. P. State Archives, Lucknow.
14. *Ismat*, January, 1910, p. 7. *Taalim-i-Niswan* by Sultan Jahan Begum, as quoted in Jaswal, G.M., op. cit.
15. *Indian Social Reformer*, Vol. 10.1899, p.266 as quoted in ibid., p.771.
16. Graham, G.I., *The Life and Work of Syed Ahmed Khan*, C.S.I., Idarah-I-Adabiyat-I-Delli, Delhi, 1974.
17. Syed Ahmad Khan to Moulvi Tasadduq Husain, in William Theodore de Bary (ed.) *Sources of Indian Tradition*, pp. 744-45 (Columbia: Columbia University Press, 1958) as quoted in Tahera Aftab, 'Negotiating with Patriarchy: South Asian Muslim Women and the Appeal

to Syed Ahmad Khan', *Women's History Review*, Vol. 14, No. 1, 2005, p.79.

18. Robinson, Francis, *Separatism among Indian Muslims: the Politics of the United Provinces, 1860-1923*, Oxford University Press, Delhi, 1993, p. 108.
19. *Minhaj al Taleem*, a book published by the Literary Society, Bareilly (1870) says, 'once women would learn to read and write they no longer would be under the control of men; would become very clever and would entertain immodest expectations; will communicate with letters and thus honour and family name would be at stake and subsequently much chaos would spread out.' Vernacular Tract No. 4303, OIOC, British Library, p. 32, as quoted in Tahera Aftab, op. cit.
20. Sir Syed's lecture on 'Progress of Muslim Women's Education', 20th April 1894, *Aligarh Institute Gazette*, 15th May, 1894.
21. Extract from the evidence of Sir C.E. Trevalyan in J.R. Richey (ed.) *Selections from Educational Records* II (1840-59) p.34.
22. 'Mohammadan Female Education', *Aligarh Institute Gazette*, 1867, No. 40, Vol. II.
23. Correspondence from Moulvi Syed Ahmad Khan Bahadur, CSI, to the Secretary, Scientific Society, Allygurh, London, 15th October 1869, *Aligarh Institute Gazette*, 1869, No.52, Vol. IV.
24. *Aligarh Institute Gazette*, 26th November, 1869.
25. Evidence of Saiyyid Ahmad Khan to the Education Commission of 1882 as given in Appendix to the Education Commission Report 1884 (Central Provinces). See also 'Sir Syed answers to the Education Commission 1882', *Aligarh Institute Gazette*, No. 62, Vol. XVII.
26. Ibid.
27. Ibid.
28. *Saiyid Ahmad Khan Ka Safar Nama-e-Punjab*, ed. Moulvi Syed Iqbal Ali, Aligarh Institute Press.
29. Ibid.
30. *Aligarh Institute Gazette*, 8th July, 1870. See also Ayesha Jalal, *Self and Sovereignty, Individual and Community in South Asian Islam Since 1850*, Oxford University Press, 2001, pp. 69-72.
31. Muhammadan Educational Congress, 1888, speech of Syed Ahmed Khan, p. 118.

32. Bhatnagar, S.K., *History of the M.A.O. College, Aligarh*, 1969, p.78. Mr. Theodore Beck came to Aligarh on 20th November 1883, but took charge of his office on 1st February 1884 on the departure of Mr. Siddons. He remained Principal of the College for more than 15 years, till his death on 2nd September 1899.

33. Abdullah, Sheikh Muhammad, *Mushahadat Va Ta'asurat*, Female Education Society, Aligarh, 1969, p.205.

34. Ibid.

35. Ibid., Ghulam-us-Saqlain belonged to Meerut but settled in Lucknow. He founded the Akhvan-us-Safa at Aligarh in 1890, an association to promote physical and moral reform. Of great independence of mind even as a student, he was active in the Muhammadan Educational Conference, and in 1891 had seconded a resolution passed in the Conference to establish a Muslim girls' school. After his graduation he maintained his links with the M.A.O. College by frequent visits, continued participation in the Union and the Akhwan-us-Safa, and articles in the magazine. He was a lawyer and a journalist by profession. Cf. Francis Robinson, *Separatism Among Indian Muslims*, p.370 and also David Lelyveld, *Aligarh's First Generation*, pp. 290-91.

36. Kauser, Nasreen, 'Muslim Women's Education in the Nineteenth Century: A Study of the Traditionalist Attitudes,' *Proceedings of the Indian History Congress*, Calicut University, 1976.

37. Aftab, Tahera, 'Negotiating with Patriarchy: South Asian Muslim Women and the Appeal to Syed Ahmad Khan', *Women's History Review*, Vol. 14, No. 1, 2005. p. 81.

38. Abdullah, Sheikh Muhammad, *Mushahadat Va Ta'asurat*, Female Education Society, Aligarh, 1969, p.206.

39. *Khatoon* edited by Sheikh Abdullah. Article by Nawab Mohsinul Mulk, 1905, No. 3, Vol. 2, p. 116. Mohsinul Mulk Mehdi Ali (1837-1907) settled in 1893 in Aligarh after resigning from the post of Financial and Political Secretary to the Nizam of Hyderabad. He revived the *Tahzib-ul-Akhlaq* and the *Aligarh Institute Gazette*, played a big part in the College Debating Society and infused new life into the Muhammadan Educational Conference. He was Secretary of the Board of Trustees, M.A.O. College, from 1898 to 1907, and Joint Secretary of All India Muslim League, 1906-07. His major aim was the continuation of the policies set out by Syed Ahmed Khan. Cf. Francis Robinson, *Separatism Among Indian Muslims*, p. 397.

Chapter IV

Female Education Section

Early Discussions, 1896-1904

It may be presumed that Syed Ahmed Khan's attitude and views regarding female education represented those held by a large section of the Muslim community during the 1880s and 1890s. But at the same time there were others among Syed Ahmed Khan's contemporaries, like Hali[1] and Justice ShahDin,[2] who, according Sheikh Abdullah, thought otherwise. The two had the co-operation of many other like-minded persons. However, the kind of opposition these persons faced can be gauged by the attitude taken by Syed Ahmed Khan, already noted. It would be of interest to examine in detail the efforts made by the reformist group to justify Muslim women's education. The history of these efforts by the supporters of women's education belonging to the Aligarh Movement is significant as we know that a movement for social reform must be first acceptable in order to be successful. This movement for Muslim female education was initiated during Syed Ahmed Khan's lifetime, but was intensified only after his death, and in the 1900s the Aligarh Movement went beyond the aims of its founder and began to promote imparting of modern education to girls through schools.

Though Syed Ahmed Khan and a number of his close associates like Bashiruddin[3] and Maulana Nazeer Ahmed opposed the spread of modern education among Muslim women, it failed to dampen the spirit of the men convinced of the need of schools for Muslim women. They continued to make efforts in that direction. Though the efforts made were not spectacular, they are significant because they form a point of departure from the conservative or traditional attitude – a break from the influence of the group formed by Syed Ahmed Khan and some of his close associates.

As already noticed, the first move in this direction was made in the Muhammadan Educational Congress in 1888 when a resolution was passed to establish schools for Muslim girls.[4] The resolution was proposed by Sheikh Khairuddin[5] and seconded by Khalifa Imaduddin[6], District Inspector of Schools, District Muzzaffargarh. During the years 1889 and 1890, nothing was done for Muslim women's education, and it seems the resolution which was drawn up in 1888 was not acted upon as there is no mention of the opening of any new school in the reports of the Educational Conferences. Again in 1891, a resolution was proposed by Moulvi Syed Karamat Hussain[7] and was seconded by Ghulam-us-Saqlain. The resolution reads as follows:

> The Conference feels that according to the conditions prevailing, Muslims should work for the education of women side by side with the men, since the advancement of the community depends on this. The education should be such that it advances the religious, literary and cultural life of women, so that with their education the future generations would stand to gain.[8]

The year 1896 is significant in the history of the educational advancement of Muslim women. For the first time, a special section called the Female Education Section of the Mohammadan Anglo-Oriental Educational Conference was created. The members of the female education section were (1) Aftab Ahmad Khan, (2) Sultan Ahmad Khan, (3) Haji Mohammad Ismail Khan, (4) Mohsinul Mulk, (5) Moulvi Bahadur Ali, (6) Moulvi Syed Mumtaz Ali, editor of *Tahzib-i-Niswan*, Lahore. Of the six members three, i.e. Haji Mohammad Ismail Khan, Mohsinul Mulk and Moulvi Mumtaz Ali,[9] seem to belong to a generation older than the rest. Educated in the traditional system, they even so seem to have a sympathetic view regarding Muslim female education. Their agreeing to become members of the Section is an indication of their comparatively liberal attitude in this respect. At the same time, let us remember that they were basically very conservative people and were opposed to any radical steps like the establishment of schools for the Muslim girls. Moulvi Mumtaz Ali is known to have subsequently opposed Sheikh Abdullah's efforts to establish a girls' school at Aligarh, while Mohsinul Mulk refrained from openly supporting him in this endeavour. Mohsinul Mulk did not even permit Sheikh Abdullah to present a resolution for the establishment of a girls' school at Aligarh in the Muhammadan Anglo-Oriental Educational Conference in 1904. On the other hand, the three younger members[10] of the Section were persons who had completed their education at Aligarh during the period Theodore Beck was the Principal of the M.A.O. College and exercised great influence over the students. It was during this period, when these three were students at the M.A.O. College, that the Siddon's Union Club had passed a resolution rejecting Syed Ahmed Khan's negative views on women's education. It, however, is significant that the Committee excluded from its membership two vociferous proponents of female education, Sheikh Abdullah and Ghulam-us-Saqlain. Another young product of M.A.O. College excluded from this Section was Syed Sajjad Hyder,[11] who appears to have been included in it sometime around 1902 and subsequently remained an enthusiastic supporter of Sheikh Abdullah in his endeavours to establish a girls' school at Aligarh. One explanation of these exclusions could be that the conservative set, forced to concede the point that a separate Section for looking after the needs of female education was needed, wanted to ensure that this forum is not used by more 'radical' elements to push any programme unacceptable to the majority of the members of the Conference.

Mohsinul Mulk was unanimously declared President and Moulvi Syed Mumtaz Ali the Secretary of the Female Education Section. The President of this Section in his speech[12] pointed out that the Female Education Section was very necessary and essential, and declared that it was obligatory on the part of all Muslims to direct their attention towards female education. "Because" he added, "the building (*imarat*) of the progress of the entire Muslim community will never be completed if its foundations i.e. female education was not strong enough." In other words, there was a need to educate Muslim women, as the community could not make true progress unless the mothers of the future generations were properly enlightened. Through a formal resolution, this Section also approved of the two resolutions that had been passed in the third (1888) and sixth (1891) sessions of the Muhammadan Educational Conference and declared that it would ensure the implementation of these resolutions. The resolution also provided for the pooling together of information regarding the situation with respect to the education of Muslim women in different localities. To facilitate this it was suggested that committees be set up in every city and town to collect details concerning women's education under the following three heads:[13]

- Government *zenana* schools.
- Missionary *zenana* schools.
- Traditional methods of educating Muslim women.

This information was to be transmitted to the Conference every five years through the delegates. Even prior to the establishment of the Female Education Section in 1896, information of this kind was received from time to time by the Conference. As early as 1886, in the First Annual Conference, there is information in the proceedings of the Muslim Educational Conference regarding the situation of education of Muslim girls at Jabalpur, furnished by one Moulvi Syed Ali Ahmad, Advocate President, Anjuman-i-Islamia. In the third and fourth Annual Conferences, in 1888 and 1889 respectively, such information was received mainly with regard to the situation in the Punjab. It is clear that the Punjabi Muslims took lead in making arrangements for educating girls. The earliest attempt by any section of the Indian Muslims to make arrangements for educating Muslim girls came from the Punjab where they established local organisations, with the designation Anjuman-i-Islamia, to provide 'suitable' education for Muslim girls and boys. As already discussed in Chapter 2, the schools of Anjuman-i-Islamia were established in the Punjab in the eighties to counter the influence of the missionaries who, it was widely believed, were using their schools for converting boys and girls to Christianity. It is specifically mentioned in the report on Punjab, published in the proceedings of the Muslim Educational Conference of 1889, that the education sought to the imparted to Muslim boys and girls through the schools run by Anjuman-i-Islamia contained a religious component so as to save them from the influence of other religions.[14] The education imparted by the Anjuman-i-Islamia organisations was highly approved of by the 'progressives' among the Muslims, for example Sheikh Khairuddin and Khalifa Imaduddin, who proposed and seconded the resolution regarding Muslim girls' education at the Muhammadan Educational Conference held in Lahore in 1888.

Despite the encouraging statement made by the President, Mohsinul Mulk, about the importance and need for the Female Education Section founded in 1896, it seems to have languished, and did not meet formally again until 1905 when the Conference was held at Aligarh. This impression is created by the absence of any proceedings of the Section from the published records of the Muhammadan Anglo-Oriental Educational Conference for the years 1896 to 1904. However, it would not be fully valid to assume that this Section remained in abeyance throughout this period. From Begum Abdullah's biography we know that in 1902 Sheikh Abdullah was elected a member and Secretary of the Female Education Section by its younger members Aftab Ahmad Khan, Sultan Ahmad Khan, Syed Sajjad Hyder and a few other old boys of the M.A.O. College.[15] Sheikh Abdullah, of course, does say that at this time these persons did not attach much significance to this Section, and as the Section existed only in name and no one was willing to work for it, they unanimously elected him its Secretary. We are in the dark about Mohsinul Mulk's and Moulvi Mumtaz Ali's reaction to this appointment, as there is no record informing us whether they accepted or objected to Sheikh Abdullah's appointment. They probably accepted the appointment in terms of their indifferent attitude towards the Section.

It seems that in the years 1897 and 1898 the members of this Section did take steps to collect information under the heads specified in its resolution passed at the first meeting. It seems the proposals and demands put across in the resolutions relating to women's education passed by the Muhammadan Anglo-Oriental Education Conference in 1899, 1900, 1901 and 1903 were apparently based on the information collected and informal discussions held by the members of this Section. In the Muhammadan Anglo-Oriental Educational Conference held at Calcutta in 1899, a resolution was passed to the effect that

> in every capital of the Provinces and in every centre of learning, a girls' school may be opened which would conform to the culture and tradition of Muslims and that this work should be completed within three years from January 1900. Moreover, in every Province, a Provincial Committee is to be set up to look after the management of the schools. And the Ulema should draw up a syllabus for girls that should conform to the tenets of Islam.[16]

For the first time, in 1900, the Muhammadan Anglo-Oriental Educational Conference deviated from its earlier stand and sought to introduce subjects like mathematics, history, geography, medicine and morality in the syllabi of Muslim girls' education.[17] Hitherto only subjects like religion and morality and sometimes domestic sciences were taught to the girls.

An important change in the character of the movement seems to have come with the passing of this resolution. For the first time it was acknowledged that besides religion and morality, a study of subjects like mathematics, medicine, history and geography was also essential 'for the spread of knowledge and progress of civilization among Muslim girls'.[18] This was a welcome change from the old stereotyped syllabus followed hitherto. Also here we find the beginnings of the acceptance of the principle that instruction merely in religion and morality did not amount to wholesome education; that together with it, some secular subjects should also be taught for the overall development of the mind.

While accepting this change, the members were cautious enough to ensure that separate text books were written for Muslim girls so as to serve their educational needs.[19] From what Chowdhury Khushi Mohammad says in his speech at the Conference[20] we may generalise that it was the opinion of the members that books being taught in schools were based on misrepresentation of facts and have a bad effect on the pupils. The reason given for women's education lagging behind was that no suitable books on secular subjects were available for them, and so long as 'good books' were not written for girls, the resolution for the establishment of girls' schools would remain a paper agenda.

It is interesting to note here that while the members of the Muhammadan Anglo-Oriental Educational Conference debated on the need and urgency of Muslim female education during their annual meetings and passed resolutions regarding female education, they at the same time ignored women in the sense that they neither encouraged their membership nor participation in the discussions of the Conference. While discussing female education, a question so vitally affecting women's position in society, the women themselves had no say in the decisions taken about them. This in itself partly explains why there was so much of theorising and little practical result from the endless discussions regarding Muslim female education. As the work of the Conference extended to other parts of India, to Madras and especially to Bombay, we find that for the first time North Indian conservatism was exposed to the liberal and emancipating influences that were becoming more prominent under the impact of modern education and of western liberalism in general in these regions. In the coastal regions, as compared to North India, the educated Muslims were less conservative and had recognised the need for female education much earlier. The coastal regions were exposed to the liberal influences at a comparatively earlier stage.

Schools for Muslim girls were already in existence in Bangalore since 1867 and in Madras since 1882.[21] The Herbert Girls' School in Madras was established by the Government for the education of Muslim girls and it was by and large not opposed by the Muslims. This contrasts with the attitude of the Muslims in North India, and especially those connected with the Aligarh Movement, who down to 1904 were debating the benefits or disadvantages of school education for Muslim girls. That the demand for girls' education was increasing in Madras is evident from the resolution passed by the Muhammadan Anglo-Oriental Educational Conference at its session held there in 1901 demanding the establishment of another girls' school in the Madras City.[22] In the Herbert Girls' School girls were taught domestic science, handicrafts, and needlework, and prizes were awarded to every successful student after the yearly examinations.[23] There is no mention of any instruction in religion being given to the girls, though there was full facility of purdah in the school. Covered carriages were provided to take the girls to and from the school.[24] In 1901 about 100 girls were receiving education in that school. The school was built in the memory of

Lady Herbert who had sanctioned Rs.10,000 for the same though the government had subsequently taken it under its control. But it seems that the arrangements existing in this school were not fully approved by the delegates attending the Muhammadan Anglo-Oriental Educational Conference held in Madras in 1901. Among these delegates obviously there were also people hailing from the Madras city itself. The main thrust of their criticism of the working of the school, as reflected in the speech of Sultan Mohiuddin, was that "some of the rules of the Herbert School went against Muslim culture which consequently did not attract girls from 'good families.'" He does clarify in his speech what those specific rules were which deterred 'good families' from sending their girls to that school. Apparently the reservation that the movers of the resolution had about the rules existing in Herbert Girls' School was of a marginal nature. On the whole they were quite satisfied with its performance. Moulvi Abdul Jabbar who seconded the resolution went out of his way in expressing that so far as girls coming from ordinary Muslim families (as distinct from those of 'good families') were concerned it was an ideal institution.[25] It seems, unlike Sultan Mohiuddin, he rated very highly the arrangements for teaching of domestic science, handicrafts and needlework in this school.

The Muhammadan Anglo-Oriental Educational Conference held in Bombay in 1903 under the Presidentship of Badruddin Tyabji was still more remarkable from the point of view of the growth of liberal attitudes among the members of the Conference over the position of women in society. For the first time women were allowed to participate in the discussions of the Conference. But, of course, they spoke from behind the purdah. This brought its quota of gossip from the conservative sections of the society. The ladies were said to be trying to make holes in the blinds and to peep at men through them![26]

This attempt at introducing the practice of allowing women to participate in the discussions of the Conference can partly be attributed to the personal influence of Badruddin Tyabji, the President of the Conference, known to hold liberal views regarding the status of Muslim women. In his inaugural address to the Conference [27] he attributed the backwardness of Muslims largely to their religious and literary prejudices and the absence of female education. He also added that Muslims had lagged behind because of the restrictions of the purdah, which had been extended far beyond the demands of the *shariat*. "I have not been able to discover anything in the Quran which either directs or even sanctions the system of purdah in all its strictness as it obtains amongst us at the present day."[28]

The Bombay Conference incidentally offered an opportunity to some of the women to speak out to men and demand their rights to advance and progress which had been denied to them by forcing on them a purdah system which transgressed the limits imposed by the *shariat*.[29] In her lecture Miss Nasiruddin suggested that arrangements should be made for Muslim ladies to attend meetings of the Muslims. Badruddin Tyabji strongly supported her in her demand.[30] Atiya Fyzee[31] and Zehra Fyzee also took an active part in the Conference.[32]

The Conference held in 1903 in Bombay passed a resolution to the effect that a girls' school should be established in accordance with the customs and practices (including purdah imposed by the *shariat*) of 'respectable' Muslim families. The resolution was passed after a lot of bickering and misgivings over the question of purdah. A heated discussion followed as to whether 'purdah', a 'religious' question, should be discussed in an educational Conference. The unanimous decision was not to discuss it in the Conference.

By 1903 the necessity of women's education had been generally accepted as a principle, but so far there had been no implementation of the suggestions made during the Muhammadan Anglo-Oriental Educational Conferences. After Sheikh Abdullah became the Secretary of the Female Education Section of the Muslim Educational Conference he tried to revive the Section and do some concrete work as regards female education. In accordance with the resolution passed in the Bombay Conference in 1903, Sheikh Abdullah wanted a resolution passed in the Lucknow session in 1904 for the establishment of a school at Aligarh. But he was dissuaded by Mohsinul Mulk from passing such a resolution at the Conference and was advised to hold a separate meeting for the same. The plea given was that since female education was unpopular, it would alienate people even more from the Aligarh Movement if such a resolution were to be tabled at the Muhammadan Anglo-Oriental Educational Conference.[33] The resolution to establish a school for girls in Aligarh was, however, passed in a separate meeting chaired by Justice Shah Din.[34]

It was also resolved that together with the meeting of the Female Education Section, an exhibition of the handmade arts and crafts of the Muslim women was to be held every year. This exhibition was given the name of Khadija Exhibition House, apparently to blunt possible criticism by conservative elements that it was a deviation from established cultural norms. The first exhibition of its kind was held in 1904 during the Muslim Educational Conference held in Lucknow. The exhibition was organised by Sultan Arabi, an old Aligarian and an advocate of Aligarh. Though the response from the Muslims was poor, a sum of Rs.868 was collected. A few 'respectable' ladies had recognised the benefits of such an exhibition and had sent their exhibits for display. To mention a few of them, they were Begum of Bhopal, Miss Fyzee,[35] Begum Sahiba Jangira, ladies from the family of Sardar Mohammad Yaqub, CIE, Prime Minister of Khairpur, Begum Syed Ahmad,[36] Sikander Jahan Begum, Waheed Jahan Begum, Sayeed Jahan Begum and Shaukat Jahan Begum from Delhi.[37] The exhibition gave rise to a spate of criticism from contemporary vernacular newspapers. The low level of this criticism can be gauged from the often-repeated remark that 'the exhibition of Muslim women's handiwork would lead in no time to the exhibition of women themselves.'[38]

With the advent of Sheikh Abdullah into the scene as Secretary of the Female Education Section, the cause of female education received a great boost. One concrete result of the efforts towards female education was that a considerable group among the Muslims had come to regard the education of women and their progress as important. The supporters and sympathisers of female education sincerely wanted to bring Muslim women to the level of their own culture and progress. The group that favoured female education believed that Muslim men could not make true progress, nor could they be really religious or deserve to be so called, unless their own women became educated.[39]

On the other hand, there were two shades of opinion prevailing among men who opposed female education. The first group believed it to be a great sin to impart education to women.[40] Their greatest objection was that educated girls would not be obedient to their husbands and they would get out of the control and influence of their families. According to them education would lead to the discarding of *purdah*, which, in their estimate, was tantamount to the ruin of the girls.[41]

The other group was not as thoughtless in its opposition. It comprised a small circle of intellectuals associated with the Muhammadan Anglo-Oriental Educational Conference who had been debating the problem of female education since 1886. This group acknowledged the importance, necessity and benefits of female education but held that the time was not yet ripe for it, and to bolster their argument they would often refer to Syed Ahmed Khan's utterances supporting their contention. In doing so, quite understandably, they would frequently refer to Syed Ahmed Khan's recorded as well as unrecorded remarks expressing his opposition to the idea of imparting modern education to Muslim women. Tufail Ahmad, a close friend and collaborator of Aftab Ahmad Khan from the very beginning, and a staunch supporter of female education in the twenties and thirties, till 1910, opposed any school for girls. In his speech[42] opposing the resolution[43] passed in the 1910 Session of the Female Education Section that girls be sent to Government Training Schools, and that three scholarships be instituted for the same, he said that as girls did not need any degree or diploma, they did not need any college education nor training in any school either. He considered the home and family to be their school and college, where girls could obtain such education as was enough for them, namely management of the household, upbringing of children and their grooming. He cited the example of Syed Ahmed Khan's mother and said that she did not receive any school or college education.

The manner in which the supporters of female education tried to counter the above objections makes interesting reading. An interaction of tradition and modernity comes into play here. The supporters of female education, when faced with a criticism of their attitude sought to be justified by frequent references to Syed Ahmed Khan's well-known views on women's education, felt quite vulnerable. They tried to counter this criticism by citing the *hadis* and examples from early Islamic history. They cited examples of the great educated ladies from the early Islamic period when the Caliphs took interest in women's education. They also frequently cited the well-known *hadis* that it was incumbent upon men as well as women to acquire knowledge. Side by side, they continued to resort to the often repeated argument that for the overall progress of the Muslim community and progress of men in general it was imperative that Muslim women be educated, for it is at the mother's feet that children first get their education. It was also highly desirable, they further argued, for compatibility in married life, for educated men would naturally want educated wives. This rather simplistic argument might have had great appeal for the persons involved in the Aligarh Movement on account of their deep commitment to the idea of ensuring modern education for as large a number of Muslim young men as possible. While conducting this kind of a debate, the supporters of female education fully respected the tradition of purdah and emphasised that Muslim women could be educated without giving up purdah. The opponents did not have anything sensible to say against this.

References

1. Altaf Hussain Hali (1837-1914) was born in Panipat and traditionally educated. He was a teacher in the Anglo-Arabic school. A younger contemporary and sympathiser of Syed Ahmed Khan, he advocated educational reform for the women behind the purdah. He was above all a poet. His son, Sajjad Hussain, a graduate from M.A.O. College, served for some time as sixth master in the M.A.O. School at Rs.60 a month. Incidentally, it was Sajjad Hussain, a student then, who had introduced the cautiously worded resolution in favour of female education in the home. Cf. Francis Robinson, *Separatism among Indian Muslims*, p.431. See also Saleha Abid Hussain's *Yadgar Hali*, Aligarh, 1949.

2. Justice Mian Mohammad Shah Din (1868-1918) was born in Lahore. He graduated in 1887 from Government College, Lahore, and in 1890 obtained his degree in Law from London. In 1893 and 1913 he was President of the All India Mohammadan Anglo-Oriental Educational Conference. In 1896 he was a Trustee of the M.A.O. College, Aligarh. In 1917 he was appointed Chief Justice of the Punjab Chief Court. A supporter of Muslim female education, he advocated the establishment of schools for Muslim girls. Cf. Bashir Ahmed, *Justice Shah Din – His Life and Writings*, Feroz Sons, Lahore, 1962.

3. Muhammad Bashiruddin founded the *Al Bashir* (Etawah) in 1899. The paper was strongly opposed to the Congress and attacked the Government when Muslim interests appeared to be ignored. By 1921 the paper had to be closed down. During its twenty-two years of existence *Al Bashir* was regarded as one of the most influential papers in the province and a reliable guide to conservative Muslim thinking. A close associate of Syed Ahmed Khan, Bashiruddin was the Manager of the Islamia School, Etawah, the most highly regarded Muslim High School in the province and a stepping stone to Aligarh.

4. Muhammadan Educational Congress, 1888, Resolution No. 17, p. 110.

5. Sheikh Khairuddin in 1888 was Head-Clerk of the office of Traffic Superintendent, N.W. Railways, and a member of Anjuman-i-Islamia, Lahore. Cf. Muhammadan Educational Congress, 1888.

6. Khalifa Imaduddin in 1888 was District Inspector of Schools, Muzaffargarh. Cf. Muhammadan Educational Congress, 1888.

7. Syed Karamat Hussain (1852-1917) belonged to Allahabad, studied Arabic and then western languages and sciences and completed his education in England being called to the Bar in 1889. From 1891 to 1897, in addition to his legal practice, he taught law at Aligarh for Rs.300 per month, a post to which he was succeeded by Aftab Ahmad Khan. A great supporter of female education, he succeeded in establishing a girls' school in Lucknow in 1912. See Hamid Ali Khan, *Hayat Maulana Karamat Hussain*, Lucknow; and also Francis Robinson, op.cit., p. 401.

8. Muhammadan Educational Conference, 1891, Resolution No. 6, p. 79.

9. Moulvi Syed Mumtaz Ali an *alim* and an advocate of women's rights within Islam, was born and educated in Deoband in Arabic and Persian. He was the editor of an Urdu journal for women *Tahzeeb -i-Niswan*, Lahore 1898, and a supporter of Muslim female education. *Makatib Sir Syed Ahmad Khan*, edited by Mushtaq Hussain, Union Printing Press, Delhi, 1960, p. 135.

10. Aftab Ahmad Khan, Sultan Ahmad Khan and Bahadur Ali were young graduates of M.A.O. College, Aligarh, holding responsible posts. Aftab Ahmad Khan (1867-1930) graduated from Aligarh and obtained his L.L.B. degree from Cambridge. In 1890 he founded the Duty Society at Aligarh. From 1905-17 he was Honorary Joint Secretary of the Muslim Educational Conference. In 1920, he became the First Vice-Chancellor of the Aligarh Muslim University. In 1923 he was President of the All India Muslim Educational Conference. Sheikh Abdullah was his chief supporter. See Francis Robinson, op. cit., p. 403, and also Habibullah Khan, *Hayat-e-Aftab*, Allahabad, 1947.

    Sultan Ahmad Khan joined College in 1886 in Ist year LL.B. He became Trustee of M.A.O. College in 1897, and later Chief Justice of Gwalior. Tufail Ahmad, *Muhammadan College Directory* (1875-1911).

Bahadur Ali joined College in 1889. He was also Trustee of M.A.O. College and became the first Secretary of the Old Boys' Association in 1901. Ibid.

11. Sajjad Haider graduated from M.A.O. College in 1901. He was Secretary of the Union Club as well as a senior prize holder. He was also Assistant Political Officer-in-charge of former Amir of Kabul, Dehradun, and a member of the Old Boys' Association. Ibid. Lelyveld writes that he was Ghulam-us-Saqlain's successor as student-intellectual in residence; See David Lelyveld *Aligarh's First Generation*, p.250.
12. Muhammadan Anglo-Oriental Educational Conference, 1896. Speech by the President, Female Education Section, pp. 244-245.
13. Muhammadan Anglo-Oriental Educational Conference, 1896, p. 63.
14. Muhammadan Educational Conference, 1889, pp. 56-60.
15. Abdullah, Sheikh, *Sawanih-Umri, Abdullah Begum*, 2nd Edition, Delhi, 1954.
16. Muhammadan Anglo-Oriental Educational Conference, 1899, Resolution No. 7.
17. Muhammadan Anglo-Oriental Educational Conference, 1900, Resolution No. 3, p. 127.
18. Ibid.
19. Muhammadan Anglo-Oriental Educational Conference, 1900, Resolution No. 3.
20. Ibid. p. 127.
21. The exact date of the establishment of the school is not known. However, the school was in existence in 1882, as is known through Mr. Ruzza Khan's testimony before the Educational Commission of 1882.

    Evidence of Mr. Ruzza Khan before the Education Commission of 1882 (Madras).
22. Muhammadan Anglo-Oriental Educational Conference, 1901, Resolution No. 14, p.314.
23. Ibid. Speech Moulvi Abdul Jabbar, p. 325.
24. Muhammadan Anglo-Oriental Educational Conference, 1901, Speech Moulvi Abdul Jabbar, p. 325.

25. Muhammadan Anglo-Oriental Educational Conference, 1901, Speech Moulvi Abdul Jabbar, p. 325.

26. Sheikh Abdullah, *Sawanih-Umri Abdullah Begum*, 2nd Edition, Delhi, 1954, p. 19.

27. Muhammadan Anglo-Oriental Educational Conference, 1903, President's inaugural speech, p. 71.

28. Hussain B. Tyabji, *Badruddin Tyabji – A Biography*, Bombay, 1952, p. 311.

29. Muhammadan Anglo-Oriental Educational Conference, 1903, speech by Miss Susie Sohrabjee, p. 130, and Chand Bibi, p. 146.

30. Hussain B. Tyabji, op. cit., Bombay, 1952. Miss Nasiruddin is identified by Hussain B. Tyabji as belonging to Timur family, p. 314.

31. Atiya Fyzee – a niece of Justice Badruddin Tyabji, was the youngest of the three sisters, Zehra Begum and Nazli Begum. After completing school at the young age of 14-15 years, she was sent to England for higher studies in Philosophy and culture. She married an artist Mr. Fyzee Rahim, who before embracing Islam was a Jew known as Mr. Reuben. Atiya Fyzee was a rigorous, brilliant and energetic person, who took an active interest in Muslim female education. She was also closely connected with the then ruling family of Bhopal.

    Cf. *Khutut-e-Iqbal banam Atiya Fyzee*, translated by Dr. Manzoor Abbas Naqvi Aligarh 1974; see also Nawab Sultan Jahan Begum. *An Account of My Life*, translated by C.H. Payne, Vol. III, pp. 43-58. Also based on an Interview with Begum Mohd. Habib.

32. Sheikh Abdullah, *Sawanih-Umri Abdullah Begum*, pp. 19-20.

33. Ibid., p. 23.

34. Ibid.

35. Sheikh Abdullah has not thrown much light on these ladies. Miss Fyzee probably belonged to Lucknow itself and seems to be educated and much westernised considering that she was known as 'Miss' Faiz as referred to by Sheikh Abdullah. The 'conservative' Muslims considered it highly improper to use western titles and much so by women.

36. Begum Syed Ahmad can probably be identified as Syed Ahmad Khan's wife.

37. Sikander Jahan, Waheed Jahan, Sayeed Jahan and Shaukat Jahan Begum were Begum Abdullah's sisters who consistently extended all help to Sheikh Abdullah and Begum Abdullah in their efforts at establishing a girls' school at Aligarh.
38. Sheikh Abdullah, *Sawanih-Umri Abdullah Begum*, op. cit., p. 29.
39. Muhammadan Anglo-Oriental Educational Conference, 1904, Annual Report of the Female Education Section, presented by its Secretary, Sheikh Abdullah.
40. Muhammadan Anglo-Oriental Educational Conference, 1905, p.183.
41. Muhammadan Anglo-Oriental Educational Conference, 1907, p. 144.
42. Muhammadan Anglo-Oriental Educational Conference, 1910, speech of Saiyid Tufail Ahmad, p. 331.
43. Muhammadan Anglo-Oriental Educational Conference, 1910, Resolution No. 1, p. 329.

CHAPTER V

A School for Muslim Girls at Aligarh

The discussions that took place in the Muhammadan Anglo-Oriental Educational Conference (earlier designated as Muhammadan Educational Conference/Congress) between 1886 and 1903 prepared the ground for the establishment of a Girls' School at Aligarh having links with the M.A.O. College. In this process, a decisive contribution was made by an enthusiastic band of young men educated at Aligarh who were active in the Female Education Section of the Muhammadan Anglo-Oriental Educational Conference. Amongst them the more important persons, besides Sheikh Abdullah, were Syed Karamat Husain, Khwaja Ghulam us Saqlain, Sajjad Haider and Abdur Rahman Bijnori.[1] The help and encouragement that these people received from Sultan Jahan Begum, the ruler of Bhopal,[2] was also a very important factor, eventually facilitating the establishment of a girls' school at Aligarh in the teeth of opposition not only from the conservative Muslims in general but also from a considerable section of the people involved in the Aligarh Movement.

The Girls' School established by Sheikh Abdullah at Aligarh in December 1906 was only one such instance of people connected with the Aligarh Movement, in one or the other capacity, trying to build exclusive institutions for girls with an aim to promote modern education among Muslim females. Sultan Jahan Begum of Bhopal established the Sultania Girls' School at Bhopal in 1903. Another school for Muslim girls was established by Karamat Husain at Lucknow in 1912.[3] Similarly, schools exclusively for Muslim girls were established in other places like Allahabad, Rampur and Agra. To identify the factors that facilitated the growth of these institutions and the problems they faced, particularly on account of the opposition from the traditional sections of the Muslim community, it would be interesting to examine the history of the girls' school at Aligarh in detail, as a case study. Aligarh, being the nerve–centre of political and ideological movements influencing the Muslim community in India during this time, such a study would enable one to discern the interplay of contending tendencies in sharp focus. Secondly, comparatively speaking, there is readily available much more information about the school at Aligarh from Sheikh Abdullah's Memoirs, the biography of his wife, the weekly journal *Khatoon*, the proceedings of the Muhammadan Anglo-Oriental Educational Conference and some of the original records preserved in the Aligarh Muslim University archives, than about other places.

No one individual has contributed more for the promotion of Muslim female education than Sheikh Abdullah. An early disciple of Syed Ahmad Khan and a graduate of M.A.O. College, Aligarh, he settled down in Aligarh to practice law although he devoted most of his time to the cause of Muslim women's education. Sheikh Abdullah came from a Kashmiri Brahmin family. He was born in June 1874 in a small village, Bhantani, in the Poonch district. He was named Thakur Das. His paternal grandfather, Mehta Mastram was a Lambardar (Village Headman). According to the practice of the time, Thakur Das commenced his education in Persian, after which he attended a maktab in Poonch, which he had to trek 4-5 miles to reach. There, in addition to Persian, he was taught Sanskrit.

Sometime then he attracted the attention of Hakim Nuruddin, court physician to the Maharaja of Kashmir, when the Hakim came to Poonch to treat a member of the royal family. The Hakim offered to take Thakur Das to Jammu and train him in Unani medicine. The boy's family reluctantly consented. Hakim Nuruddin was a leading Qadiani, and under his tutelage, Thakur Das converted to the Ahmadiya sect and took the name Sheikh Abdullah. That year the Mohammedan Educational Conference had its convention in Lahore where, for the first time, Sheikh Abdullah heard Sir Syed and his followers. With the Hakim's aide, he travelled to Lahore for his secondary education and later to Aligarh for college and law school. In 1891, he passed the Matriculation Examination, and came to Aligarh with a letter of introduction from Hakim Saheb to Sir Syed. He was admitted to the first year. He took active part in debates and discussions and various activities like drill, cricket, football and horse riding. In 1896, he won the Cambridge Speaking Prize, which was awarded to the best debater by the Union. At Aligarh, Sheikh Abdullah became a Sunni Muslim, thereby declaring his independence of his patron.[4]

He often had the opportunity of meeting Sir Syed and talking to him. He acknowledged that it was Sir Syed who inspired in him an interest in writing. Besides, the affection of Sir Syed and his modern ideas awoke in him a desire to serve the community. Sir Syed often entrusted boys with responsibility; the names of Aftab Ahmad Khan and Sheikh Abdullah figured among them. Because Sheikh Abdullah in a way spiritually identified with the Movement, he was appointed as librarian. He carried out that assignment until he completed his education. When he had completed his L.L.B., Principal Beck, who was also the Secretary of the Movement, suggested that he should set up practice in Aligarh. Sheikh Abdullah accepted his suggestion, stayed on, and also became active in the Old Boys' Association.[5]

Sheikh Abdullah found his real substitute family at Aligarh. He became a member of the Duty Society, comprising a select group of Aligarh students, and founded by his friend, Aftab Ahmad Khan. This Society helped raise money for the College and embodied the ideas of social service and community leadership dear to Sir Syed. The brotherhood of Aligarh students and *alumni* provided Sheikh Abdullah with a network of friends, allies, and patrons, the support system normally provided by one's extended kin. Sheikh Abdullah, though a convert, was well accepted by his peers and elders in the Aligarh Movement, as evidenced by those who arranged his marriage, and by the large group that attended the *nikah*. He had adopted the faith of Islam; in turn a cross section of the North Indian '*ashraf*' adopted him as their own.[6]

As already noticed, Sheikh Abdullah was already active in the Muhammadan Educational Conference, which in 1896 had started a Female Section, of which Sheikh Abdullah became Secretary in 1902.[7] In the same year he married a young woman, Waheed Jahan, from an old Mughal family of Delhi in which women's education was a tradition.[8] Her father, Ibrahim Mirza, had taught his daughters Persian and Urdu and had also permitted an English woman to teach them. Together, both Sheikh Abdullah and Begum Abdullah campaigned for a girls' school in Aligarh. Sheikh Abdullah had the strength of character to stand up to his beliefs and do what he thought right regardless of public opinion, 'but not to the point of ostracism'. He is said to have possessed the 'unique combination of independence and realism.'[9]

He had personally witnessed the oppression of women and his heart bled for their plight. When the convention of the Muhammadan Educational Conference was held in Delhi in 1902, he mustered up his friends and proposed that the Section for Female Education should be rejuvenated.

Once he was made Secretary of the Female Education Section of the Muslim Educational Conference he started working towards reviving that Section and looked for ways and means to draw the attention of the Muslims towards female education.[10] In this drive Begum Abdullah's contribution cannot be overlooked. Sheikh Abdullah started the girls' school and took care of all the external work, but without Begum Abdullah's cooperation, sympathy, sacrifice and hard work, it would have been impossible to establish a boarding school, especially in those times. It was only because of the active interest she took in the boarding school and her participation that it was a success.[11]

The idea of a school for Muslim girls took shape in 1903 in Bombay during the Muhammadan Anglo-Oriental Educational Conference, where it was resolved that a normal school for Muslim girls should be established.[12] But the venue of the school was not decided in the Conference. Sheikh Abdullah corresponded with Maulana Mumtaz Ali, Editor, *Tehzeeb Niswan* (Lahore) and Mehboob Alam, Editor, *Paisa Akhbar*, (Lahore) to establish a normal school at Lahore. But he received disappointing letters from both.[13] It was then that he undertook upon himself the stupendous task of establishing a school for Muslim girls in Aligarh.

To elicit public opinion, he asked Begum Abdullah to call a conference of educated ladies in her house to discuss the problem of Muslim female education. A conference was called where many educated ladies gathered, prominent among them being Mrs. Razaullah Khan and Sayeed Ahmad Begum. The women at the gathering were unanimously in favour of female education. The very idea of such a conference led to criticism in the locality. It was rumoured that henceforth the ways and methods of the English would be practiced and schools would be opened for girls where they would not observe purdah etc. It was also alleged that in the proposed school, 'good' and 'bad' girls would meet, which would be detrimental to the interests of girls coming from 'good and decent families.' Moreover, fears were also expressed whether such a school would succeed in giving proper training in 'Islamic culture and decency.'[14]

However, all this criticism did not deter Sheikh Abdullah and he devoted himself to writing articles in newspapers focusing on the need for female education.[15] Some people supported his views but a large number of Muslim intellectuals worked against Sheikh Abdullah's scheme to establish a girls' school at Aligarh and published articles against the stand Sheikh Abdullah had taken.[16] People expressed doubt as to whether Islamic culture and traditions would be maintained at all in this new institution. A large majority was of the opinion that this was a severe deviation from Islam. It was widely circulated that girls from 'noble families' would be sent to schools where they would interact with their counterparts from all kinds of families, thus endangering their character. These schools for women could become the cause of moral degradation for women. The saddest part pertained to apprehensions regarding the veil; not only men but orthodox women also mourned the loss of it.[17]

Instead of being discouraged by such criticism, in 1904 Sheikh Abdullah took a bold step and instituted a magazine entitled *Khatoon* for mobilizing public opinion in support of women's education and the general welfare of women.[18] He was supported in this effort by Syed Sajjad Haider, Syed Abu Mohammad, Moulvi Ehteshamuddin and Moulvi Enamul Haq.[19] The first issue of *Khatoon* came out in July 1904 and it created a furore in Urdu journalistic circles. Other magazines and newspapers began opposing its publication. Some said that *Khatoon* was a '*naturi*' magazine and was being published with the aim of abolishing purdah.[20] One moulvi, steeped in conservative tradition, accused that any magazine published from Aligarh was bound to be the antithesis of religious beliefs. He further alleged that Syed Ahmad Khan had taken upon himself the task of uprooting Islam through educating men and now his disciple is thinking of exterminating the same through educating women.[21] The hostile propaganda against *Khatoon* alarmed Mohsinul Mulk, who was then Secretary of the Board of Trustees, M.A.O. College. He advised that the publication of *Khatoon* be stopped, as, according to him, its continuance could harm the cause of the Aligarh Movement.[22] But he was brought around and made to understand by Sheikh Abdullah that it was not so, and he became so convinced[23] that he too began contributing articles to the magazine.[24] *Khatoon* continued to be published till 1914 and ceaselessly fought for its goals.[25] It had influenced considerably a large section of men and women in favour of Muslim female education by then.

An important landmark in the efforts for the establishment of a girls' school at Aligarh was the sanction of a grant of Rs.100 p.m. by the Begum of Bhopal in 1904 towards the expenses of such a school at Aligarh.[26] To begin with, Mohsinul Mulk did not appreciate this idea at all, for according to him, the people of Aligarh were creating enough trouble because of the M.A.O. College, and it would be impossible to live there if a girls' school was also established. Sheikh Abdullah gives a vivid picture of Mohsinul Mulk's reaction when he came to learn of the grant from the Begum of Bhopal. When informed of the sanctioning of this grant by the Begum of Bhopal, showing great anger, he threw his cap on the ground in full view of many visitors impressing upon them that Sheikh Abdullah had done something that went against his wishes. But afterwards he told Sheikh Abdullah with a smile to carry on with his work, adding that it was also necessary that people should know that he (Mohsinul Mulk) was not in favour of the establishment of any school for Muslim girls.[27] Mohsinul Mulk also refused permission to propose a resolution in the Muhammadan Educational Conference in 1904, in Lucknow, for establishing a girls' school at Aligarh.[28] Sheikh Abdullah persuaded a few friends to hold a separate meeting (in support of starting a *madrasa* for girls in Aligarh). Such a meeting, comprising of 150-200 people, was held in a small house in Qaiser Bagh, presided by Justice Shah Din. Sir Theodore Morrison also participated in the meeting. The resolution was passed in the meeting, including a vote of thanks for Begum of Bhopal's munificence.[29] Such were the times that it had not been possible to even propose such a resolution in the Muhammadan Anglo-Oriental Educational Conference. The resolution to establish a girls' school at Aligarh was, however, unanimously approved in the All India Muslim Ladies Conference held in Aligarh in December 1905.[30]

The leaders of the Aligarh Movement initially gave no encouragement, moral or financial, to the movement for female education pioneered by Sheikh Abdullah. Mohsinul Mulk refused permission at the last moment to use any building of the M.A.O. College to hold the Muslim Ladies Conference and the exhibition of women's handicrafts.[31]

Later it became known that some conservative people had warned the authorities of the College that if the Conference took place in any of the houses on the campus, the public would get too unruly. Although the Society's house was about three quarters of a mile away from the College, it still remained the property of the College. That was the reason of the objection and why the Conference could not be held there as planned.[32]

After much difficulty, a building known as Shahpoorji Kothi was rented, which became the venue of the exhibition and the Women's Conference.[33] The exhibition was a success and the Female Education Section gave a standing ovation to Sheikh Abdullah for his outstanding efforts. This was too much for people like Shaukat Ali, who, at the close of the meeting, accosted Sheikh Abdullah and assaulted him.[34] Though Shaukat Ali was no opponent[35] of women's education, he, it seems, resented the credit going to Aftab Ahmad Khan's 'group'.[36] This incident showed that often opposition to the establishment of a girls' school also stemmed from personal or factional rivalries within the Aligarh Movement.

The magazine *Khatoon* played a great role in the success of the exhibition and the function. For the exhibition, more than a hundred pieces of excellent embroidery had arrived from Lahore, Delhi, Meerut, Agra, Moradabad and other places. Her Highness, Nawab Sultan Jahan Begum showed her interest in the success of the Exhibition, which is evident from the *farman* dated 30th Sept. 1905 that she sent written by her Secretary on her behalf. She also showed her practical involvement by sending two oil paintings made by her and a few pieces of embroidery.[37]

The ladies who participated actively in the Conference were of the Fyzee and Tayyabji families from Bombay. The youths who helped in making the Exhibition successful were Maulvi Ehteshamuddin saheb; Mr. Abdul Rehman Siddiqui Khan saheb, Buniyad Husain saheb; Mr. Zahoor Ahmad saheb, Barrister at Law, Allahabad; and the late Maulvi Imamul Haq saheb. Begum Abdullah and her sisters were the soul of the Women's Conference. Her keen interest and involvement made such an impact on the ladies who came from other places, that they returned home with a desire to attend women's conferences in future as well.[38]

During early 1906, as the question of finances for the proposed school became the prime concern, a fund raising campaign was initiated with the then students of Aligarh. Abdur Rahman Siddiqui,[39] Syed Buniyad Husain, Mr.Zahoor Ahmad, Abdur Rahman Bijnori, and Syed Mahmood, went around Kathiawar, Bombay, and Hyderabad to collect annual subscriptions. Mrs. Neyaz Ahmad of Meerut and Miss Atiya and Zehra Fyzee of Bombay figured prominently in collecting considerable sums. In 1906, the total amount collected as donation for the normal school in Aligarh in different ways, including the donation of the Begum of Bhopal, was Rs.13,838 and 11 annas plus Rs.100 monthly as donation from Bhopal.[40]

As the sources of finance were very meagre, it was considered necessary to apply to the State Government for financial help.

Sheikh Abdullah wrote an application to the Lt. Governor of U.P., Sir James Latouche, stating that the education of Muslim women was neglected and asked permission for a deputation to be allowed to meet the Governor in order to ask for financial help for a girls' school in Aligarh. A petition was also sent, and the Lt. Governor agreed to meet the deputation on 2nd May 1906.[41] Six members, out of a deputation of nine members, backed out at the eleventh hour, and only three were left to meet the Governor. They were Raja Naushad 'Ali Khan,[42] Khwaja Ghulam us Saqlain and Moulvi Muhammad Naseem.[43] The reasons for the reluctance on the part of the prominent Muslims included in the deputation to associate themselves with the efforts for soliciting government patronage for the girls school is an indication of strong social pressure that existed against the movement. Some persons, mostly local landowners, had agreed to be included in the deputation as it was an opportunity to meet the Governor, but on second thoughts considered it safer not to be associated with the move.[44] In any case, Sheikh Abdullah was able to make out a convincing case before the Governor for a school for Muslim girls in Aligarh. The Governor promised to consider the request for the grant favourably only after such a school was actually started and, after due inspection, also favourably reported on by the Inspector of Schools.

Gradually the results of Sheikh Abdullah and Begum Abdullah's hard work bore fruit and within three months about fifty girls began attending the school. Sheikh Abdullah informed the Lt. Governor who arranged to send Miss Ganja as an inspectress to assess the situation and report to him.[45] She came at the appointed time, and confided in Sheikh Abdullah that the inspection was just a formality to be gone through, so that the *madrasa* could get a grant from the government. When she saw the dedication and involvement of Begum Abdullah and her sisters, she was impressed and said that they were doing the kind of work that is usually associated with missionaries. Within a month after the receipt of Miss

Ganja's report, Sheikh Abdullah received a sealed envelope from the Government. It contained a letter of appreciation saying that his Highness was extremely pleased to read the report and had approved a grant of Rs. 250 per month and Rs.17,000 specifically for the infrastructure.[46]

References

1. Abdur Rehman Bijnori, was a civil servant in Bhopal. A student of Aligarh, he was expelled from the M.A.O. College after the 1907 college strike, but allowed to return later. He conceived the Sultania College project. Cf. Francis Robinson, *Separatism Among Indian Muslims*, p. 369.
2. The Begum of Bhopal, who was a great supporter and sympathizer of Muslim female education, had established a girls' school in Bhopal in 1903, called the Sultania Girls' School. 140 students were enrolled in the first year of the school and all were under 10 years of age. Subjects such as Arithmetic, Geography, Domestic economy, together with Urdu and the Quran with its translations were taught. There was full arrangement of purdah in the school. Cf. *An Account of My Life* Nawab Sultan Jahan Begum, Vol. II, translated by Major Abdus Samad Khan, Bombay, 1922, p. 152.
3. Karamat Husain opened a Muslim girls' boarding school in Lucknow in 1912. Besides being given moral and religious education, the girls were taught Urdu, Persian, Arabic, English and Arts and Crafts. There was full arrangement of purdah in the school. Karamat Husain donated a sum of 2 lakhs to the school. Cf. *Hayat Karamat Husain*, pp. 161-166.
4. Minault, Gail, 'Sheikh Abdullah, Begum Abdullah, and Sharif Education for Girls at Aligarh' in Imtiaz Ahmed (ed.) *Modernization and Social Change among Muslims in India*, Manohar Publications, 1983. p. 211. See also Saiyid Tofail Ahmad, *Mussalmanon ka Roshan Mustaqbil*, Delhi, 1945, p. 228.
5. *Biography of Begum Abdullah* by Padma Bhushan Khan Bahadur Sheikh Abdullah; Translation Atia Abid, Aligarh University Press; Introduction.
6. Minault, Gail, op. cit., p. 211.

7. Abdullah, Sheikh Mohammad, *Sawanih-Umri Begum Abdullah*, Kohinoor Press, Delhi, 1954, p. 17. The ancestors of Mirza Ibrahim Beg were Mughals who had maintained traditions of learning and government service during the transition to British rule. Mirza Ibrahim Beg was a minor municipal official in Delhi and a supporter of Sir Syed's educational movement. He sent his only son Bashir Mirza to Aligarh College where he was a classmate of Sheikh Abdullah. Mirza Ibrahim also educated his four daughters, himself teaching them Urdu and Persian at home and inviting an English woman to come and instruct them in Arithmetic and elementary English. Wahid Jahan, though purdah- observing, thus had a good vernacular education, a smattering of English, and in addition wrote a fine hand.
8. *Sawanih-Umri*, op. cit., pp. 6-8.
9. Minault, Gail, op. cit., p. 212.
10. *Sawanih-Umri*, p. 18.
11. Ibid., p. 4. See also pp. 108-112.
12. Muhammadan Anglo-Oriental Educational Conference, 1903, Resolution No.5, p. 5.
13. *Sawanih-Umri*, p. 20.
14. Ibid., pp. 18-19.
15. Ibid., p. 19.
16. Ibid., p. 19. See also Tufail Ahmad, *Mussalmanon Ka Roshan Mustaqbil*, p. 228.
17. *Biography of Begum Abdullah*; p. 15.
18. *Sawanih-Umri*, p. 21.
19. Ibid.
20. Ibid., p. 22.
21. Ibid.
22. Ibid., p. 23.
23. Ibid.
24. 'Right and Duty'; article by Mohsinul Mulk, *Khatoon*, edited and published by Sheikh Abdullah, March 1905, No.3, Vol. II, p. 116.
25. *Sawanih-Umri*, p. 23.

26. Ibid., p. 25 See also Sheikh Muhammad Abdullah, *Mushahadat Va Ta'ssurat*, Female Education Society, Aligarh, 1869, p. 221, and Tofail Ahmad, *Mussalmanon Ka Roshan Mustaqbil*, p. 228.

27. Sheikh Muhammad Abdullah, *Mushahadat Va Ta'ssurat*, pp. 221-223. This narration shows the ambiguous policy followed by Mohsinul Mulk. It seems that at this time even Aftab Ahmad Khan, who later became an enthusiastic supporter of Sheikh Abdullah, was against the establishment of a girls' school at Aligarh, p. 221.

28. *Sawanih-Umri*, p. 27.

29. Ibid. See also *Mushahadat Va Ta'ssurat*, p. 222.

30. *Khatoon*, published and edited by Sheikh Abdullah, 1906, January No. 1, Vol. 3, p. 12.

31. *Sawanih-Umri*, p. 30.

32. *Biography of Begum Abdullah* by Padma Bhushan Khan Bahadur Sheikh Abdullah. Trans. Atia Abid, Aligarh University Press; p. 29.

33. Ibid.

34. *Mushahadat Va Ta'ssurat*, pp.180-189.

35. *Muhammadan Anglo-Oriental College Magazine*, 15th January, 1900. Shaukat Ali spoke on the need of educated wives for the new generation of educated men.

36. David Lelyveld, *Aligarh's First Generation, Muslim Solidarity in British India*, Princeton University Press, New Jersey, 1978, p. 334. For a more detailed study of factions within the Aligarh Movement, see David Lelyveld, 'Three Aligarh students, Aftab Ahmad Khan, Ziauddun Ahmad, Muhammad Ali,' *Modern Asian Studies*, April, 1975, pp. 227-240, and Gail Minault and David Lelyveld, 'The Campaign for a Muslim University' 1898-1920, *Modern Asian Studies*, VIII, April 1974, pp. 145-189. See also *Aligarh's First Generation*, Chapters VI and VII.

37. *Biography of Begum Abdullah*, op. cit., p. 24.

38. Ibid., p. 29.

39. Abdur Rehman Siddiqui was a journalist and politician by occupation. A B.A., LL.B. from Aligarh, he was the President of the Aligarh Students Union, and founder member of the All India Muslim League. He managed Mohammad Ali's affairs while he was interned and kept him in touch with politics. He was much involved with the

agitation for his release. He remained in England during the 1920s and 1930s, becoming a successful businessman: later he became Governor of East Pakistan. Cf. *Separatism Among Indian Muslims*.

40. *Sawanih-Umri*, p.34.

41. Ibid.

42. Raja Naushad Ali Khan, a landowner by occupation, held the Mailaraigunj estate in Barabanki district, paying Rs.9464 land revenue. He was Raja Jehangirabad's nephew. He attended the foundation session of the All India Muslim League at Dacca in 1906 and was appointed a member of its Provisional Committee. He was the 1st Secretary of the U.P. Provincial Muslim League after its foundation in June 1909. He faded from politics after the Morley-Minto Reforms. Cf. *Separatism Among Indian Muslims*, p.408.

43. Moulvi Muhammad Naseem (1859-1953) was a lawyer practicing at the Awadh Bar. His son, Muhammad Habib, became professor of History at Aligarh Muslim University. Naseem started practice in 1890 and from 1894 to his retirement in 1917, was regarded as the leader of the Awadh Bar. In 1909, he defeated Syed Nabiullah, Munshi Ehtasham Ali and Raja Naushad Ali Khan in the election for the Awadh Muslim seat, but then withdrew. Cf. *Separatism Among Indian Muslims*, p.411.

44. *Sawanih-Umri*. See also Tofail Ahmad, *Mussalmanon Ka Roshan Mustaqbil*.

45. *Biography of Begum Abdullah*, op. cit., p. 37.

46. Ibid., p. 38.

Chapter VI

From Female Normal School to Mohammadan Girls' School, 1906-10

On 25 October 1906[1] Sheikh Abdullah established the school in a small house in Mohalla Bala-e-Quila of Aligarh town after some alterations were done to ensure seclusion.[2] The funds collected by Sheikh Abdullah during the preceding year, including the Rs.1,200 sent by Bhopal state as the annual grant for 1905, was deposited in the account of M.A.O. College. Initially, Sheikh Abdullah had planned to deposit it in a joint-account with himself and a friend of his as signatories, but eventually it was decided that it should be deposited in the College which could in turn put it in the bank. People had been unaware of this, so when through the newspapers they were given the information, they desisted from further media campaigns. It was with the help of this small amount that a teacher from Delhi was employed and space for the school was procured. Advertisements had been given in the newspapers and letters written to friends that they try to get a lady teacher somehow, but nothing came of it. Finally they learned of the teacher in Delhi. All her conditions were accepted and she agreed to come to Aligarh only when she was allowed to bring with her, her mother, her husband and children. All of them resided in the premises of the school.[3]

It soon became apparent that the teacher was not fully qualified and it was difficult for her to carry on the teaching of even traditional subjects like recitation of the Quran and the reading and writing of Urdu language single-handedly. Because of the non-availability of a capable lady teacher, Begum Abdullah, together with her two sisters, took on the responsibility of a major part of the teaching in the school. Begum Abdullah went everyday to the school to oversee the arrangements, neglecting at times her own family. She regarded the students as members of her own family. More often than not, she went hungry herself sharing her tiffin with girls who could not afford to bring tiffin everyday. Begum Abdullah taught reading and writing Urdu. One of her sisters taught the Quran. Through the efforts of Begum Abdullah the unwilling parents were ultimately persuaded to send their children to the school. Most of the students belonged to poor families, who had sometimes to be fed and clothed by Begum Abdullah.[4] Six months later, the inspectress of schools visited the school and was happy to recommend a grant-in-aid to the school. The school received a grant of Rs.15,000 plus a recurring monthly grant of up to Rs.250.[5]

To begin with, seventeen girls were enrolled in the school. But soon most of these girls left the school as the missionaries running a girls' school at Aligarh had become jealous of Sheikh Abdullah's enterprise, and they went out of their way in persuading the parents of the pupils to shift them to their institution. At one stage the school was left with only three pupils.[6] But it seems, due to the tireless efforts of Sheikh Abdullah and his wife, soon the confidence of parents was restored. By 21 December 1906, forty-five girls had been enrolled. Four men were employed to take the girls in two carefully covered *dolis* to their homes and bring them to the school. One female peon was also employed.[7] The curriculum included Urdu reading and writing, basic arithmetic, needlework and the Quran. The school building itself was walled on all sides so that purdah could be properly observed.[8]

There existed a strong opinion even among the members of the female section of the Muhammadan Anglo-Oriental Educational Conference that, instead of establishing an ordinary girls' school, it would be preferable to have a Normal School for training female teachers who would in turn become instrumental in spreading education among Muslim women in different parts of the country. Behind this insistence was the anxiety of many persons who were co-operating with Sheikh Abdullah in promoting female education to work out a system that would ensure the tutoring of students at their homes. It appears that many of these people, finding it embarrassing to oppose the establishment of a regular school for girls, wanted such a development to be postponed by insisting that priority be given to a Normal School for training teachers. Sheikh Abdullah, on his part, was convinced that the real need was for an ordinary kind of school for imparting modern education to the Muslim girls, and he suspected that the proposal for a Normal School was only a diversion. It was obvious that unless a considerable number of Muslim girls were able to acquire formal education up to Middle standard, the candidates for training at a Normal School for teacher training would not be available.[9]

Another problem was that parents did not want to continue sending their daughters to school once they attained puberty and became marriageable. Besides, the '*sharif*' families also did not want their daughters to opt for a career in teaching.[10]

But Sheikh Abdullah had, from the very beginning, adopted an attitude of avoiding open debate on this issue. While establishing this school, he again adopted an ambiguous attitude. He designated his school as a Female Normal School, but in fact ran it like an ordinary school teaching from primary up to middle classes. This helped Sheikh Abdullah to achieve his goal without rousing suspicions of the more conservative elements among the Trustees of the M.A.O. College, in whose control the finances of the school were placed from the very beginning.[11] From the manner in which

Viqarul Mulk refers to this matter in one of his letters dated 10th May, 1909 addressed to the Peoples Bank of India, Meerut,[12] an impression is created that the placing of school finances under the control of the Trustees of M.A.O. College in 1905 was decided upon by Sheikh Abdullah and the then Secretary of Trustees' Council, Mohsinul Mulk, without the matter being ever placed before the Trustees formally. Perhaps Sheikh Abdullah feared that if this debate about the nature of the school was allowed to be conducted publicly, and if he insisted on having an ordinary kind of school, this might panic Mohsinul Mulk into disassociating the Trustees Council from the school, which could have deprived the school of the prestige that even this kind of a vague affiliation with the M.A.O. College could give to it. Thus the school, established by Sheikh Abdullah at Bala-e-Qila on 25 October 1906, an ordinary girls' school, had the facade of a Normal School and was referred to as such in the formal correspondence down to 1909.

The people who were opposed to the school and its activities tried to harass the students in different ways through the agency of the riff-raffs of the town. Sheikh Abdullah got constant complaints about the palanquin bearers being beaten, or his *madrasa* criticized, as a result of which some parents withdrew their wards. Besides, the notorious people of the locality instigated some mischievous boys who would stand at a distance from the *madrasa*, and when the palanquins approached, they would raise the curtains, exposing the girls. Everyday he had to sort out such problems. When the activities of the boys got out of hand, one morning, with a whip in hand, he hid behind a wall on the road. He himself witnessed them misbehaving and laughing. Then and there, he not only took them to task but whipped whosoever he could catch hold of. Sheikh Abdullah had to intervene and threaten the instigators with litigation if they did not stop harassing the girls.[13]

One episode relating to Sheikh Abdullah's fight of those days against persons responsible for organising provocations against the school, deserves mention. The other episode related to a Muslim *tehsildar*. A Muslim *tehsildar*, conservative and bigoted in his outlook, lived in the vicinity of the school. He was continuously trying to dissuade people from sending their wards to the school alleging that thereby the girls would be spoilt. He invented a canard that a particular girl had developed illicit relations with the driver of the *ekka* on which she went to the school. When confronted with this, Sheikh Abdullah was deeply demoralized.[14] This incident shows how backward even the educated Muslims of Aligarh were and the kind of hardships that had to be faced by Sheikh Abdullah and his collaborators in running his school.

These incidents reflect the mentality of the Muslims of Aligarh in those days because of which there were innumerable obstructions in the path of Muslim girls' education. However, despite these difficulties, gradually the strength of the students in the school gradually increased and soon the total number of students rose to fifty. Subsequently, on Sheikh Abdullah's report to the Governor of U.P. about the establishment of the school, the latter deputed Miss Ganja to inspect the school. She inspected the school and gave a favourable report.[15]

In 1905, Sheikh Abdullah had purchased fourteen *bigha* of garden land in the village, Dodhpur, for Rs.1950 from Lala Lalita Prasad Kayasth, a local landowner. After the establishment of the girls' school, Sheikh Abdullah gifted this plot for the school and hostel buildings.[16] Between 1906-1907, Rs.4053 was collected in cash, which included the contribution of a lump sum grant of Rs.300 by the Begum of Bhopal, which was in addition to her recurring grant of Rs.100 per month. The rest of the money, i.e. Rs.3753, was collected through private donations. In this collection a significant part was played by persons like Moulvi Abdullah Jan, Asif Zaman, Sahibzada Abdul Hafiz, Khurshid Ali Han, and Qazi Abdul Aziz, who took deputations to different places for raising funds for the school.[17] Among the students who helped raise funds for the girls' school were Abdur Rahman Siddiqui, Syed Bunyad Husain, Abdur Rahman Bijnori, Syed Zahur Ahmad and Syed Mahmud. Donations came from families in Bombay, from Muslim officials from States like Hyderabad, Baroda and Patiala, and other private sources.[18]

Besides this, the U.P. Government had sanctioned Rs.17,000 in cash for construction of buildings for the school and boarding house. The government had also promised to give Rs.250 per month on condition that it corresponded with the amount collected through private donations.[19] It is not clear whether the U.P. government's promised grant of Rs.250 per month was contingent upon the school raising an equal amount per month from private sources or it meant that the government shall pay to the school any amount up to Rs.250 per month that would be equal to the steady income per month of the school.

In the meantime, Sheikh Abdullah purchased more land contiguous to the plot in village Dodhpur that he had gifted to the school in 1905. He used, for this purpose, the amount of Rs.17,000 sanctioned by the government for the construction of buildings for school and boarding house.[20] The total area of the land so acquired grew to about forty *bighas*. A road was constructed through the efforts of Sheikh Abdullah and others between the railway station and the village Dodhpur during the time Marris was the Collector of Aligarh District, and the lands on both sides of the road were divided into plots and sold for residential purposes. The area around this road, which was designated Marris Road after the name of Marris, soon became a prestigious locality. The land which had been a wilderness when Sheikh Abdullah purchased it in 1905, now became a part of the this prestigious Marris Road area.[21]

With the passage of time the Trustees of the M.A.O. College became more intimately involved in the running of the school, which was a great protection for those who were running it in the face of the growing hostility of the conservative elements among the Muslims. In 1907, when the opponents of the school conducted a press campaign casting suspicion on the manner in which the amount, given by the government, was being utilised, Sheikh Abdullah, in his rejoinder, stated that the funds of the school were deposited in the bank in the account of the M.A.O. College, Aligarh.[22] This is also corroborated by the rough draft of a letter by 'the Honorary Secretary, M.A.O. College,' to the Manager of the People's Bank of India, Ltd., dated 10th May 1909.[23] In this letter it is stated clearly that 'the Trustees of M.A.O. College are entitled to withdraw the deposit money as the Female Normal School is being run under their guidance and they are controlling the finances of the school and have got all the funds in their possession.' This evidence, taken together with Sheikh Abdullah's testimony quoted above, makes it obvious that not only were the finances of the school given under the control of the Trustees of M.A.O. College, but it also came to be run under their 'guidance' within one year of its establishment. This speaks volumes for the deftness and care with which Sheikh Abdullah proceeded in his efforts to establish a girls' school in the face of stiff opposition from different quarters and fear of some of the influential trustees of M.A.O. College about the possible adverse reaction of the Muslim community.[24] Apparently, the arrangement that had been finally agreed to between the Trustees of the M.A.O. College and Sheikh Abdullah about the running of the girls' school stipulated that while its finances would be quietly controlled by the former, the day to day running of the school would be the sole responsibility of Sheikh Abdullah and his collaborators. The Trustees of the College, in the exercise of their authority as the body establishing the school, formally appointed Sheikh Abdullah as Secretary of the School.

The tacit recognition extended by the Trustees of the M.A.O. College to the new school as an institution 'run under their guidance'[25] appears to have considerably improved its position. In 1908, grants worth Rs.150 per month were received from three native states of Khairpur, Bahawalpur and Tonk raising the total income to about Rs.500 per month. Cash grants from native states, donations, governmental and other aids amounted to Rs.18,564.[26] The popularity of the Female Normal School of Aligarh spread far and wide, for Sheikh Abdullah mentions in the Annual Report of the Female Education Section, 1908, that people from outside Aligarh now wanted to send their daughters to the school. The need of a boarding school was felt as parents withdrew their daughters once they attained the age of 11-12 years, which meant they could not study beyond Class III or IV. Consequently, efforts to educate them went waste and no concrete result could be shown to the public. A boarding school had to be established, where parents could leave their daughters to study beyond Class IV without any fear or anxiety of having to travel between school and home everyday.

The year 1909 can be termed a crucial year, a dividing line between two phases of the development of the school. We have noticed a beginning had been made in 1907 to establish formal links with the M.A.O. College through the control of the school funds by the Trustees of the M.A.O. College, and by investing in them the power to appoint the Secretary of the School who was to be the highest administrative authority in the institution. This control was strengthened and the girls' school increasingly came under the purview of the College, as is evident from the documents preserved in the Aligarh University Archives. It is also significant that the school which was designated at the time of its establishment as 'Female Normal school'[27] was designated as the 'Mohammadan Girls' School',[28] which is an indication that resistance among the Trustees of the College to having a regular girls' school having been weakened considerably, Sheikh Abdullah and other persons running the school were emboldened to give up their ambiguous stance with respect to the character and nature of the school. They were no longer afraid of its being known as an ordinary kind of girls' school meant for Muslim families. Moreover, the girls' school was to have a boarding house as well. The idea of having a boarding house was conceived sometime in 1908 and a proposal to erect a building for it on the plot located in the village Dodhpur, gifted to the school by Sheikh Abdullah, was mooted in 1909. During the same year, Viqarul Mulk, the Secretary of the Board of Trustees, M.A.O. College, requested Lady Porter, wife of the acting Lt. Governor of U. P., to lay the foundation stone of the school's boarding house. The foundation was laid on November 1911 and the construction began.[29]

The proposal for the establishment of the boarding house for Muslim girls created a sharp reaction not only among the ordinary Muslims, but even among people connected with the M.A.O. College. Strangely enough, prominent among them was the opposition of W.A.J. Archibald, the then principal of the College, and Dr. Ziauddin Ahmed.[30] Both considered the premises of the M.A.O. College to be too close to the proposed site of the boarding house which, according to them, would create mischievous consequences and which would in turn lead to defamation of both the M.A.O. College and the Girls' School. They also feared that given the proximity of the boarding house to the College, the boarding house would not attract many girls, and it would be difficult to maintain the discipline of the College. Archibald even threatened to resign on this issue. Sheikh Abdullah replied that the boarding house would be strictly a *purdah* observing one, and it would, moreover, be one and a quarter mile away from the M.A.O. College. Also, when the families of the staff of the College could live within the premises of the College without any mishap, it was unreasonable to suggest that the girls' boarding house would have any adverse effect on the discipline of the M.A.O. College. Sheikh Abdullah also pointed out that the resignation of Archibald would have no effect on the well being of the College and the College authorities should not allow themselves to be pressurized by him. Viqarul Mulk supported Sheikh Abdullah in his stand.[31] The length to which Viqarul

Mulk was prepared to go to associate himself and the Trustees of the M.A.O. College with Sheikh Abdullah's enterprise at this juncture may be gauged from the fact that around this time he appears to have accepted the position of Honorary Secretary of the Mohammadan Girls' School,[32] a position occupied by Sheikh Abdullah previously. We come to know about Viqarul Mulk holding this position from a letter by G.A. Tayler, Agent, Bank of Bengal, Agra, addressed to 'M. Mushtaq Hussain, Honorary Secretary, Mohammadan Girls' School, Aligarh,' dated 1 January 1910.

When and why this change occurred is difficult to explain because of the paucity of evidence. It is also not clear as to what was the formal position of Sheikh Abdullah after he was replaced as the Secretary of the School by Viqarul Mulk, although one may assume that this was only a formal change and for all practical purposes the school remained his exclusive responsibility. One can conjecture that the designation of Viqarul Mulk as the Secretary of the School at a time of fierce campaign against the move to build a boarding for the school, was yet another clever move on the part of Sheikh Abdullah to earn legitimacy for the school in the eyes of that large section of Muslim population who had come to accept the M.A.O. College as a symbol of their progress and prosperity. The appointment of Viqarul Mulk as Secretary of the Girls' School as well could help create the impression that the whole scheme was being executed under the personal supervision of the Secretary of the Board of Trustees of M.A.O. College.

References

1. Muhammadan Anglo-Oriental Educational Conference 1906. Report of the Female Education Section, p. 124. Sheikh Abdullah seems to be confused regarding the date of the establishment of the Madrasa in Bala-e-Qila in Aligarh. In *Sawanih-Umri* (p.39), he writes

that the school was established towards the end of the year 1906. On the contrary, in *Mushahadat Va Ta'ssurat*, p. 232, he says that the school started functioning formally in 1907, though some girls, on an informal basis began studying the Quran in 1906.The date for the establishment of the school as given in the report of the Female Education Section (1906) is 25th Oct 1906.

2. *Sawanih-Umri*, p. 39.
3. Ibid. See also Tufail Ahmad, *Mussalmanon ka Roshan Mustaqbil*, Delhi, 1945.
4. *Sawanih-Umri*, p. 40.
5. UP Education Department, 368, 1912.
6. Muhammadan Anglo-Oriental Educational Conference, 1906. Report of the Female Education Section, p. 124.
7. Ibid.
8. *Khatoon*, III, 10 October 1906.
9. *Mushahadat va Ta'assurat*, p. 212.
10. *Sawanih-Umri*, p. 41.
11. *Mushahadat va Ta'assurat*, p. 226. Sheikh Abdullah mentions that he had been depositing the funds of the school in the accounts of the M.A.O. College on the advice of Mohsinul Mulk from 1905 onwards.
12. Aligarh Muslim University Archives: File No. 51, Document No. 2.
13. *Sawanih-Umri*, p. 41.
14. Ibid., p. 42.
15. *Khatoon.*
16. *Sawanih-Umri*, p. 46.
17. Muhammadan Anglo-Oriental Educational Conference, 1906. Report of the Female Education Section, p. 144.
18. *Sawanih-Umri*, p. 52, also *Khatoon* (January-September 1909).
19. Muhammadan Anglo-Oriental Educational Conference, 1906. Report of the Female Education Section, p. 144.
20. Tufail Ahmad, *Mussalmanon ka Roshan Mustaqbil*, p. 229.
21. *Sawanih-Umri*, p. 52.
22. Ibid., p. 45.

23. Aligarh Muslim University Archives: File No. 51, Document No. 2.
24. During the 1904 session of the Anglo-Oriental Educational Conference, held in Lucknow, when Sheikh Abdullah informed Mohsinul Mulk of the grant of Rs.1,200 from the Begum of Bhopal for the establishment of a girls' school, he (i.e. Mohsinul Mulk) made a public show of anger against Sheikh Abdullah's efforts to raise resources for the planned school. Again, during the same Conference, he did not permit a resolution for the establishment of a Girls' Normal School in Aligarh to be proposed at the Conference. The resolution was passed in a separate meeting of special invitees convened by Sheikh Abdullah.
25. Aligarh Muslim University Archives: File No. 51, Document No. 2.
26. Muhammadan Anglo-Oriental Educational Conference, 1908. Report of the Female Education Section, p. 149.
27. Aligarh Muslim University Archives: File No. 51, Document No. 2.
28. Aligarh Muslim University Archives: File No. 51, Document No. 15.
29. Aligarh Muslim University Archives: File No. 51, Document No. 5.
30. *Sawanih-Umri*, pp. 49-49. Dr. Ziauddin Ahmad (1878-1947) passed M.A. in 1898 from Aligarh and obtained his D.Sc Degree in 1901 from Trinity College, Cambridge. He was also member of the Royal Mathematical Society in 1904. In 1906, he got his Ph.D. from Gottingen. He also studied in Paris, Bologna and Al-azhar in 1906-07. He joined Aligarh as Professor of Mathematics in 1907. He became Principal of the M.A.O. College in 1918, first Pro-Vice Chancellor in 1921. In 1926, he became the Vice-Chancellor of Aligarh Muslim University and remained so for the next two decades. Cf. Mohammad Amir Zubairi, *Ziya-e Hayat*. See also Francis Robinson, *Separatism Among Indian Muslims*, p. 392.
31. *Sawanih-Umri*, p. 49.
32. Aligarh Muslim University Archives: File No. 51, Document No. 15.

Chapter VII

A Degree College Managed by the University

The foundation of the Boarding House of Muhammadan Girls' School was laid in November 1911 by Lady Porter, wife of the Lt. Governor of U.P. It was planned to accommodate around a hundred and twenty-five students, with dining facilities arranged around a quadrangle, and surrounded by a double wall. The outer enclosure ensured strict seclusion, in order to preempt unfavourable opinion.[1]

The laying of the foundation stone of the boarding house was marked by a fresh wave of hostile propaganda against the School in the Urdu newspapers and magazines. In this round of criticism the lead was taken by some elements closely connected with the M.A.O. College. These people were fighting against the entrenched group of Trustees for the control of the institution. In this factional struggle, Sheikh Abdullah, being one of Aftab Ahmed Khan's young followers, stood on the side of the dominant group. To denigrate the College establishment, the oppositional faction led by Mohammad Ali, picked at Sheikh Abdullah and directed fiery criticism against him for running a regular girls' school and a girls' boarding house. Muhammad Ali raked up the old controversy of the Normal School versus the ordinary kind of school. He sharply criticized Sheikh Abdullah's work in the columns of *Com-*

rade, which he edited. Mohammad Ali accused Sheikh Abdullah of emulating the western system of education, which he thought was unfit for Indian conditions. He asserted that personally he was favourably disposed towards the establishment of a Normal or Training School for girls[2] and wanted training schools to be established so that they produced trained mistresses who could in turn be appointed in individual homes to teach the girls, and was against girls going to ordinary schools.[3] Moulvi Mumtaz Ali, editor of *Tahzeeb-Niswan*, Lahore, an erstwhile member of the Female Education Section, and a self-proclaimed supporter of the cause of female education, was another notable opponent of the girls' boarding house in Aligarh, as is evident from an article published in the *Khatoon* of March 1912, written by a 'Muslim lady'.[4] In this article Mumtaz Ali's opposition to the Boarding House is attributed to personal jealousy against Sheikh Abdullah, resulting from his failure to establish a Muslim girls' school at Lahore as agreed to in the Bombay session of the Muhammadan Anglo-Oriental Educational Conference in 1903. In his bitterness, according to the author of the article, Mumtaz Ali opposed any step taken by Sheikh Abdullah towards the establishment of a similar school at Aligarh. In any case, this campaign against the school did not prove to be very effective. The debate on the nature of the school was raised by Muhammad Ali a bit too late. An attack on the girls' school from this angle could have been effective in 1908 or 1909, when Sheikh Abdullah, apparently with the consent of Viqarul Mulk, quietly transformed the Female Normal School as it was originally conceived into the Muhammdan Girls' School. But by 1911 a majority of the Trustees had given up their reservation on this score. They had learnt from their own experience that the establishment of an ordinary kind of school for the education of Muslim girls at Aligarh did not, after all, prove to be such a great provocation to the common Muslim as it was made out by the conservative elements. The open support extended by the Governor of U.P. and the

Begum of Bhopal to the planned extension of the school, including the establishment of a Boarding House, apparently, proved to be a very important factor modifying the attitude of a majority of the Trustees in this respect. Hence it is understandable that the press campaign launched by Muhammad Ali and Mumtaz Ali against the School towards the end of 1911 proved to be a complete flop in so far as it failed to rattle the Trustees to a point that they should have considered disassociating themselves from Sheikh Abdullah's venture.

The School crossed the primary stage and entered the middle school stage in 1912. The teaching of the English language had also been introduced, although it was optional.[5] It will be interesting to note here that a resolution was proposed in the Muhammadan Anglo-Oriental Educational Conference of 1913 that full arrangements should be made to teach English in this school. The resolution was supported by Ahsan ul Haq, Barrister at Law, Sheikh Abdullah, (Dr) Ziauddin Ahmad, Aftab Ahmad, and Maulana Abul Kalam Azad. It was opposed by Zafar-ul Mulk, editor, *Al-Nazir*,[6] (Dr) Mirza Yaqub Beg, Moulvi Bashiruddin, editor *Al-Bashir*, and Abdul Ghaffar. The resolution was passed by majority vote.[7]

In 1913 the building of the Boarding House was complete. It was formally inaugurated in a gala ceremony in March 1914 by the Begum of Bhopal who had contributed Rs.20,000 towards its construction.[8] The decision to invite the Begum was taken in view of her eminence so that people would hear of it, which would give it due publicity. 'The Begum in her ribbon-cutting speech quipped that the doors of the hall which had stuck when she tried to open them, symbolized the obstacles still facing Muslim girls' education.' This school, by educating the daughters of '*sharif*' families would do much to contribute to the progress of the community. The government had aided the school, but could do little without the cooperation of the community itself. Even the Muhammadan Educational Conference, she said, would continue to pass resolutions, but do very little else, unless Muslim women became active on their own behalf. She addressed those present as educated women, who had the obligation to organize associations in their locales to raise funds for this school and other girls' schools, and to write articles and make speeches in favour of girls' education. They should also start schools, paying special attention to teacher training, religious and moral instruction and purdah arrangements. As for the question of European women teachers, she noted that many Europeans had given devoted service to Indian education, and had gained the respect and affection of their students. Muslim women should follow the example of Begum Abdullah, who, as Honorary Superintendent of the new girls' school, proved able to work well with the European woman Principal, besides providing a reassuring maternal presence to the students and their parents. The Begum also referred to two thorny questions of policy. In the matter of the Normal School, she said, Sheikh Abdullah had assured her that once the boarding school had got going, his next big effort would be to institute training classes. As for teaching English, the Begum said that 'the emphasis should be on good primary education in Urdu', but that 'for girls who wanted to go on to higher stages English would also be necessary'.[9]

To begin with, nine girls were admitted to the hostel. Among them, three were his own daughters, three were the daughters of Begum Abdullah's sister, one was Begum Abdullah's friend Maimoona Begum's daughter, and two others were from Bulandshahar (Begum Abdullah had been taking care of these girls for several years). By the end of the year, however, enrollment had risen to twenty-five, of whom sixteen were boarders.[10]

Begum Abdullah began to reside in the hostel and left her children in the care of maidservants. In those days, there was no population around the hostel, and, during the night, people were afraid to move around even within the campus. Though there were watchmen and dogs all the time, yet little girls could not be left on their own, so Begum Abdullah and some teachers stayed with them. Begum Abdullah's devotion instilled a sense of confidence among the people. Begum Abdullah sometimes invited the prospective students with their mothers to stay in the hostel and judge for themselves. The father would discuss the curriculum and the living arrangements with Sheikh Abdullah. They could withdraw their daughter if they were not satisfied. This practice went a long way in satisfying some people and they let their daughters stay.[11]

The total amount incurred on the building of this Boarding House came to Rs.60,000. According to Sheikh Abdullah, the Boarding House that started functioning from March 1914, to begin with, had only nine students as its members. But it seems soon, as a result of the selfless work of Begum Abdullah, who was made in-charge from its very inception, the reputation of the Boarding House was fully established as a safe place for the stay of girls belonging to even conservative families having great insistence on purdah arrangements. Begum Abdullah was made the Honorary Superintendent of the Boarding House, and she saw to it that "various features of utility from a Muslim point of view had been introduced in the boarding life." Religious education had been made compulsory and girls could not get promotion to the next class until they had passed their tests in the prescribed course in Theology. A room in the Boarding House had been set apart as the Prayer Room and a Muslim lady teacher had been appointed to look after all the arrangements about the regularity of daily prayers in the room.[12]

As a consequence, the number of resident students began increasing, and within two years need was felt for yet another hostel. In 1916, the foundation stone of Sultania Hostel was laid by the Begum of Bhopal.

'The daily routine of the school included early rising, lessons in the morning, more lessons plus study and rest time in the afternoon, time for exercise and games, and the five daily prayers. In addition to the regular curriculum of Urdu reading and writing, mathematics and the Quran, the girls had classes in embroidery and cooking once or twice a week. From Class III, students learned English for an hour a day, some Indian history and geography and Islamic Theology. Purdah was extremely strict. Fortress-like walls kept out all unauthorized persons, and curtained carriages transported the students on outings or to the station…' Begum Abdullah's supervisory duties included all those of a '*sharif*' woman-head of the household.[13]

> Begum Abdullah acted as a surrogate mother to all the Aligarh girl students, counseling them in moments of sorrow, nursing them when ill, treating them as her own along with her own five daughters.'

She was fondly known as 'Ala Bi' (a nickname for mother which combines both respect and affection) and Sheikh Abdullah was called 'Papa Mian' by the students who called each other 'Apa' while at school and ever thereafter. The management of the Aligarh Girls' School consciously emphasized familial and affective ties among the extended family of its students and graduates. Religious rituals at the school in addition to regular prayers included occasional *ameen* and *milad* ceremonies. The *milad* was especially popular among Aligarh girl students, which again emphasized the familial atmosphere of the school.[14]

By 1915 the Department of Education agreed to recognise the school as an Anglo-Vernacular School. A considerable number of girls were already studying English there with their parents' consent.[15] In 1915, four girls appeared in the Middle Vernacular Examinations out of which three were successful.[16] This progress of the school once again roused the dormant jealousies, and conspiracies aimed at thwarting its onward march became active at different levels. In October 1915, the Begum of Bhopal received an anonymous complaint about the school. She asked Aftab Ahmed Khan to investigate the matter in secrecy. Aftab Ahmed Khan did not let the matter come to public notice and his report, which was 'in the interest of the school', was dispatched secretly to the Begum of Bhopal.[17] During this time a more serious kind of opposition came from an unexpected quarter, the Department of Education. The Director of Education, an Englishman, adopted an unhelpful attitude towards the progress of the school. He was not in favour of any support – financial or otherwise – being given to Muslims for their education and upliftment, and was reluctant to allow the Muslim Girls' School to send girls for the Anglo-Vernacular Middle Examination, on the plea that it was just a primary school.[18] He also created difficulties for Sheikh Abdullah in the sanction of a government grant of Rs.20,000, which Sheikh Abdullah had asked for, for the construction of school buildings. Sheikh Abdullah could override these difficulties and the objections of the Director of Education as he had good contacts with Lord Meston, the Governor of U.P.[19]

There exists some indirect evidence suggesting that some time before the second half of 1917, a new society designated as Female Education Association was formed with Sheikh Abdullah as its secretary. This society, which was registered under the Education and Welfare Societies Act of 1860, had as its members Nawab Mumtaz ud Daula (Prime Minister of Jaipur), Viqar ul Mulk, Muzzamil ullah Khan and Honorable Aftab Ahmed Khan. Through the constitution of this society an attempt was made to regularise the jurisdiction that was given to the Trustees of M.A.O. College way back in 1906. 'It is the right of the Trustees of the M.A.O. College,' the constitution stipulated, 'to ask and inspect the accounts of the Association and advice and control the decisions of the Association.'[20] Thus the informal arrangement worked out earlier was given a legal form through the constitution of the Female Education Association registered in 1917. But this legalisation of the existing arrangements had a negative feature from the point of view of those who wanted the school's administration to be fully integrated with that of M.A.O. College, i.e., to make it obligatory for the College authorities to take responsibility for its finances. In the presence of clearly stated rules of a registered association defining the limited role of the Trustees in the management of the School, it was no longer possible to surreptitiously thrust any further obligation over the Trustees with respect to the School.

In 1918, the School came to be upgraded to Classes IX and X for the purpose of preparing girls for the Matriculation examination.[21] According to Sheikh Abdullah the first batch of the students of the school appeared in the matriculation examination in 1919. All the candidates were declared passed. Some of them even obtained scholarships on the basis of their performance in the examination.[22] With the opening of Matriculation classes the School was renamed Muslim Girls' High School and Sheikh Abdullah once again became the Secretary of the School. This is borne out by a draft of an application, 'Secretary, Girls' High School about 'Help'', signed by Sheikh Abdullah, which is dated March 1923.[23]

The introduction of Matriculation classes in the School in 1918-19 had led to an increase in the over-all expenditure of the School and, subsequently, for sometime it was running in deficit. To Sheikh Abdullah's disappointment the Muslim Girls' High School was not listed in the original Charter of the University enacted in 1920, as one of its maintained institutions. Had this been done, the problem of finding finances for the School would have been solved finally. But apparently the Trustees of the M.A.O. College did not consider their obligations towards the School significant enough to merit some kind of reiteration in the Act establishing the Aligarh Muslim University enacted on their advice and suggestion. To meet the deficit in school finances, efforts for raising funds were renewed on a big scale. This drive brought an additional grant of Rs.600 per annum from Bhopal.[24] The U.P. Government also 'gave temporarily a small additional help'. However, this additional income was not sufficient to meet the recurring deficit in the school budget and by 1922-23 it became indebted for an amount of Rs.3,600. In March 1923 Sheikh Abdullah, in his capacity as Secretary of the Girls' High School, wrote to the Vice Chancellor of the newly established University to give to the School a loan of Rs.3,600 for liquidating the existing debt. In this communication he also suggested that as the School had begun to send girls from that year for the Matriculation examination conducted by the Aligarh Muslim University it may be hoped that in course of time 'the University will be able to take full responsibility for its upkeep'.[25] This application carried endorsements from several members of the Executive Council like Abdul Khaliq, Habibullah Khan, and Tufail Ahmed. There are three other signatures, which are illegible.[26] It also has the signature of Mr. Wilayat Husain who was at this time office superintendent in the establishment of the All India Muslim Educational Conference.[27] On the other hand, it carries a dissenting note by Ziauddin Ahmed, the then Pro-Vice Chancellor, who had, earlier in 1909, opposed the building of the Boarding House for girls at its present site. While signing the document, which was perhaps circulated by Sheikh Abdullah for enlisting the support of the members of the Executive Council and other important persons, he added: 'I don't agree in principle.'[28]

Despite the Pro-Vice-Chancellor's opposition a loan of Rs.3,500 was granted by the Vice-Chancellor to the School with the stipulation that it should be returned by the end of the next financial year. However, the next year, the School was not in a position to pay back the loan due to unforeseen expenditures on the purchase of some more lands and purdah carriages for the students. Sometime before 22nd December 1924, Sheikh Abdullah wrote to the Vice-Chancellor asking for the removal of the time-limit for the repayment of this loan.[29] The Finance Committee considered this request at its meeting held on 22nd December1924 and recommended the extension of the period of re-payment of the loan to 31st March 1925.[30] This recommendation was endorsed by the Executive Council at its meeting held on 18 January, 1925. Sheikh Abdullah had made this request knowing fully well that Ziauddin Ahmed, the Pro-Vice Chancellor, had serious reservations about the whole transaction. But it seems that with Aftab Ahmed Khan's election as the Vice-Chancellor on 24 December 1923 the situation in this respect had changed radically. Sheikh Abdullah was very close to the new Vice-Chancellor personally, and Aftab Ahmed Khan had throughout maintained by and large a helpful attitude towards the Muslim Girls' High School.

As already noticed, the formation of the Female Education Association in 1917 was a step giving statuary basis to the organizational links that had been created as a result of the efforts of Sheikh Abdullah and his collaborators to bring the Muslim Girls' High School under the aegis of the M.A.O. College. The Female Education Association was then made the Governing Body of the Muslim Girls' High School, and its members were Trustees of the M.A.O. College, or closely connected with it. The Trustees, moreover, were given the power to advise and control the decisions of the Association. Beside this, the Secretary of the Board of Trustees was designated as the President of the Association. But it appears that this arrangement still suffered from one serious infirmity. The Trustees on their part are not known to have ever formally accepted the jurisdiction and obligations with respect to this school given to them through the constitution of the Female Education Association. Apparently, whatever responsibility was accepted by the Trustees informally, was not taken seriously by them. This is borne out by the fact that in 1920 they did not insist on the inclusion of Muslim Girls' High School in the list of the institutions maintained by the Aligarh Muslim University under Article 12 of its Charter enacted in the same year. Thus it is obvious that with the coming into existence of the Aligarh Muslim University in 1920, the frail statutory links established between the Muslim Girls' High School and the M.A.O. College in 1917 were obliterated. As a matter of fact, after 1920, any reference to the constitution of the Muslim Female Association would have been embarrassing to persons like Sheikh Abdullah who tried during the early twenties to persuade the University to accept 'the full responsibility of its up keep.' Thus in the first half of the twenties, during which time Sheikh Abdullah hoped to procure University help and recognition for the School through his personal influence, he appears to have scrupulously avoided any mention of the Female Education Association. Instead, a new body designated as Board of Women's Education was created, which perhaps had a statutory position as a Standing Committee of the Academic Council. It was empowered to deal with the problems relating to female education, which would naturally also cover the affairs of the Muslim Girls' School. This is also borne out by item 62 in the Minutes of the Executive Council of 5 July 1926, noting a resolution passed by the Academic Council on 8th February 1926 adopting and recommending to the Executive Council the Proceedings of the Board of Women's Education, dated 25 January 1926.[31] From the text of the resolution of the Board of Women's Education, dated 25 January 1926, reproduced in the above Minutes, it is obvious that this Body was not directly related to the School. It only processed the matters referred to it by the Academic Council. But it is significant to note that there does not exist evidence suggesting that this Body ever held any meeting other than recorded in the Minutes of the Executive Council dated 5 July 1926. The only plausible explanation for this could be that this Standing Committee of the Academic Council existed only for a brief period. It was possibly created sometime after the establishment of the Aligarh Muslim University to regulate the University's links with Muslim Girls' School. The greater likelihood seems to be that it was created after Aftab Ahmed Khan's taking over of the charge of the office of the Vice-Chancellor in January 1924 and it became defunct with his exit in 1926. Apparently such a Standing Committee with the high sounding designation of Board of Women's Education was created under Sheikh Abdullah's inspiration. As we have already noticed, Sheikh Abdullah was very influential during this period on account of his proximity to the Vice-Chancellor. He apparently wanted to have this kind of a statutory committee to make up for the gap created by the obliteration of the links visualized in the constitution of the Female Education Association between the Muslim Girls' High School and the M.A.O. College, as a result of the enactment of the Charter of the University which excluded the School from the list of its maintained institutions. From the above quoted Minutes we also get the impression that Sheikh Abdullah sought to use it for securing University assistance for this institution after it had been raised to the level of an Intermediate College in 1925. It is also possible that the decision to open Intermediate classes in 1925 was taken in the Board of Women's Education, but in the absence of any firm evidence this can only be a conjecture. Aftab Ahmed Khan's resignation from the Vice-Chancellorship of the University in 1926, in a situation when Sheikh Abdullah was no longer in a position to procure informal help and recognition of the University for his school by manipulating the Board of Women's Education, seems to have motivated him to revive the Female Education Association. That this was done to emphasize the jurisdiction and responsibilities that had been entrusted to the authorities of the M.A.O. College, the parent institution of Aligarh Muslim University, is clearly borne out by the manner in which the constitution of the Female Education Association was sought to be reintroduced in 1929 under the garb of the 'Qawaid' (Rule) of the School and Intermediate College.[32]

It seems that after reviving the Female Education Association, sometime around 1926, Sheikh Abdullah succeeded in persuading the University authorities to accept the same kind of authority and obligations towards the Muslim Girls' School/Intermediate College that were given in the constitution of the Female Education

Association to the Trustees of M.A.O. College. This was sought to be achieved through resolutions of the Executive Council[33] and Academic Council,[34] dated 12th May and 13th May 1929, nominating the Vice-Chancellor and Pro-Vice-Chancellor to 'the Muslim Girls' Intermediate College Managing Committee', which was in reality the Managing Committee created by the constitution of the Muslim Female Association. The language of these resolutions was carefully drafted to make it clear that the Vice-Chancellor and the Pro-Vice-Chancellor would be members of the Managing Committee not in their capacity as the representatives of the University as such, but only as those of the Executive Council and Academic Council respectively. Moreover, care was also taken to ensure that recognition was not extended to the Female Education Association as a result of the mention of its name in the resolution.

This arrangement, in any case, subsequently, paved the way for further integration of the Muslim Girls' High School/Intermediate College with the University set up. According to Tufail Ahmed, sometime in 1929, the Girls' College received an annual grant of Rs.1200 from the University. In March 1937 the University Executive Council sanctioned yet another lump-sum grant of Rs.5000 but its payment was made contingent upon the Muslim Girls' Intermediate College fulfilling certain conditions. In November of the same year, these conditions were waived and the amount of the grant was allowed to be disbursed to the College forthwith. It was for the first time that the University had made such considerable financial commitments towards the maintenance of the Muslim Girls' High School/Intermediate College. It is quite understandable that while making these financial commitments, the University authorities would also be inclined to exercise powers, already entrusted to them, for regulating the administration of the institution. In the Minutes of the Executive Council, dated 28 November 1937, under item 236, there is, for example, recorded a sanction of the temporary appointments of three lady teachers with effect from

16 October 1937. This was an unprecedented decision in the sense that until this date the Executive Council of the University had not been invested with powers to make appointments to the staff of the Muslim Girls' High School/Intermediate College. Although the Executive Council did enjoy the power, under the provision in the constitution of the Female Education Association giving the Trustees of the M.A.O. College authority to 'advice and control the decision of the Association', the Executive Council could have in practice stretched this power to include appointments only with the full cooperation of the Managing Committee of the Muslim Girls' High School/Intermediate College.

The substantial assistance given by the University during the thirties appears to have made the financial position of the Muslim Girls' High School/College much better. The College did not receive help from the 'Native States' from 1933 onwards. The only regular income other than the U.P. Government's grant, and that of the University, that the School/College continued to receive after 1933 was the annual help of Rs.250 offered by the Muhammadan Anglo-Oriental Educational Conference.[35] Despite the discontinuation of all grants other than those of the U.P. Government and the University, the Muslim Girls' High School/Intermediate College was able to substantially increase the freeships, stipends and other facilities of the deserving students. The School/Intermediate College was in a position to give twelve scholarships in the shape of freeships to deserving and poor girls. Girls admitted as free boarders were charged nothing at all for their tuition, lodging etc., and in addition were given extra help to provide for their other expenses. Parents and guardians of girls to be admitted as free boarders were required by the school authorities to give e definite undertaking in writing that girls so admitted shall not be removed from the school before they had passed at least the Middle Examination.[36]

It was again in the 1930s that Sheikh Abdullah and others collaborating with him began the planning for degree classes in the

College. A proposal to this effect was for the first time mooted in 1934 from the platform of the Muhammadan Anglo-Oriental Educational Conference. The Conference passed a resolution suggesting arrangements for B.A. degree classes in the Intermediate Girls' College, and requested the community for funds for implementing this suggestion.[37] Subsequently, in 1936[38] and 1937,[39] the Conference reiterated this appeal. In 1938, the B.A. classes were introduced in the Girls' College.[40] The opening of the Degree classes from July 1938[41] was a turning point in the history of the Girls' College, for, not only was the Intermediate College now raised to the status of a Degree College, but more important, the institution succeeded in achieving what it had been striving for, for so many years, to obtain a large measure of integration with the Aligarh Muslim University. In the meeting of the Executive Council held on 17 July 1938, it was resolved that 'the Degree Classes of the Muslim Girls' College be taken over from the present session and be incorporated in the University as part of the Departments concerned.'[42] It was also resolved in the subsequent Executive Council meeting that 'a New Hall be created for the residence of women students joining Degree Classes and be located for the present in the Muslim Girls' College,'[43] and that 'before the building is started, proper legal agreement be executed with the Girls' College authorities on the understanding that the building will belong to the University.'[44] It was also arranged in 1938 for girls to attend the Aligarh Muslim University Training College, where full facility of purdah was maintained. Seven girls were enrolled in the first year.[45] The hostel arrangements for these girls, who were enrolled directly as students of the University, were left to the authorities of the Women's College. Those of them, who were boarders, were accommodated in the newly erected Women's Hall.

The teaching of the science subjects was introduced for the girls at the Intermediate and B.Sc. level in 1942.[46] As women teachers were not available, arrangements were made for the sciences subjects to be taught by male lecturers. For this purpose, the Department of Science of the Women's College was to take full advantage of the University laboratories.[47]

These developments show that, in 1938, for all practical purposes, the Girls' School and Intermediate College and the Girls' College at the Degree level became separate entities, with the latter under the control of the University. But in 1942 the reluctance of the University to accept the Girls' High School and Intermediate College under its fold was finally overcome and the Girls' School and College became the maintained institutions of the University under Section 12 of the Charter.[48]

The Women's College, by this time, had established itself as a credible institution for women's education and had succeeded in removing to some extent the prejudice regarding the need for women's education. The Women's College has been enjoying the dual benefits of receiving grants and financial sanctions through the mother body, while at the same time enjoying semi-autonomous status, ever since the take-over by the Aligarh Muslim University. Also, the Women's College has permanent representation in the Academic Council, Executive Council and the AMU Court.

Over the years the Women's College has nurtured other institutions of female education in the city – the Girls' High School, the Senior Secondary School and two schools of the primary section. Its credible functioning as a full-fledged institution has led to the recognition of the Girls' High School as a separate unit. This was soon followed by the Senior Secondary School for Girls. Each of them function as semi-autonomous units.

The College is also known as Abdullah Girls' College, after its founder, Sheikh Abdullah. The strength of the College was well over 2,600 in 2006. Twenty-nine courses of study are offered under the canopy of five faculties in the College. The students enrolling in the College are given a series of Orientation Lectures at the beginning of the session to familiarize them with their surroundings.

These lectures primarily aim at discussing the history, customs and traditions of the College, in addition to imparting awareness of women's rights, career building and health related issues.[49]

To cater to the needs of the students, the College has big and spacious classrooms, laboratories, a ground for sports activities and an auditorium for supporting extra-curricular activities.

The Bachelor Degree course in Commerce for girls was shifted from the Department of Commerce to Women's College in 1999. The addition of Geology in the Honours Programme in the Women's College was one of the very important decisions taken in 2002. The teaching of Communicative English at the undergraduate level (as a step towards acquiring a PG degree in ELT later) is a unique opportunity offered by the College to its girls. In the same spirit, courses in Functional Urdu and Hindi are also being run on a subsidiary level at Women's College.[50]

Furthermore, subjects like Women's Studies, Tourism, and Library Science are also offered to girls in keeping with the demands of the time. Though new courses of study like Geology and Women's Studies have been introduced to enhance the choices available for women to excel in, the College needs to introduce many more courses which will not only attract more students to the College, but also offer a vast number of areas from which students can pick their careers.

The Women's College teaching programme implicitly follows all the academic programmes formulated and passed by the Board of Studies of the different Departments of Studies. The proposal to change over to the UGC initiative of pre-structured courses was adopted at the Women's College also. The Home Science undergraduate and post-graduate programmes were reformulated with special care and new ordinances were framed and passed to suit the re-formulations. The aim of teaching is envisaged as building a new feeder group for Higher Education and Research Programmes in the country. The plan of action is for Women's College to stay tuned to the developments in the Departments of Studies in the University in terms of restructuring of syllabi, course content etc.

As per information for 2006, the student strength of the College stood at 2560 spread over five faculties. Teaching staff stood at 112; Permanent: 97; Temporary: 09; Guest Faculty: 30. Student-teacher ratio worked out to be 2560:112=23:1.[51] The number of seats per subject is kept at a minimum because of the shortage of facilities. The College upholds a high standard of teaching which is clearly indicated by the annual results every year. In all faculties, the Abdullah College girls regularly figure in the top ten ranks. Thus the girls, supported by a team of dedicated and talented teachers, are venturing into new fields of knowledge. This is truly empowerment of women through education.

Women's College has come a long way, but aims to accomplish a lot more in the coming years in order to be acknowledged as a bastion of women's education in the modern times, as it did earlier.

Conclusion

The success of Sheikh Abdullah's efforts in the form of the growth of the School into the College and its integration with the M.A.O. College, Aligarh Muslim University, is clear indication that the problems of women's education had assumed a character which was not merely local. It was now a problem that was national in scope, and formed a major part of the struggle for women's emancipation. Participation through financial aids or efforts to win public approval, as also to gain sufficient attendance in the already existing institution at Aligarh, came from areas that were widespread. For example, as has already been suggested, the decisive factor in the very existence of the School was the financial aid given by the Begum of Bhopal. Her ceaseless involvement with the School brought to the forefront more radical issues like a Boarding House for women. This necessarily meant that for the first time women would be venturing outside their homes and participating in a process that with time would become more collective. The opening of the Boarding House then enabled women from all parts of the country to live together and participate more fully in the process of educating themselves. It meant essentially that a way was being opened for women themselves to become a motive force in the movement for their education.

The venture was then in this sense an effort at modernity. It was an effort, however, that at every stage kept in view public approval, as also the values of traditional society. In other words, care was taken to see that the accepted institutions of Muslim society were not seriously challenged. To do so, would have meant the failure of their venture. Their deep understanding of the problems involved in bringing women into the mainstream of national life, therefore, made them keep pace with the changes in other aspects of their social life. They could not have proceeded at a faster or more radical pace than they did. Religion in particular was not to be violated. All their concepts and actions were justified on the basis of traditional values. *Purdah* was never questioned. The study of the Quran formed an integral part of the curriculum, and Persian and Urdu were still emphasised. Though women were also to be trained as teachers, the main purpose of education was still stated as traditional, in the sense of educating women to become better wives. In other words, education was to enable them to adjust to the now more educated men. The force of this tradition was such, that the Girls' School could not be publicly declared an ordinary school until 1910. The idea of an institution for women could not have been accepted until then, another factor which shows that the movement had every stage to proceed in accordance with public approval.

The education system, therefore, could further the emancipation of women only in a very limited sense. As such, some of its characteristic features, which have been discussed, would seem to us today very conservative. But seen within the light of the problems it had to contend with, as also the social system within which it had to function and which it eventually helped change, it was truly a radical step. For its time, it was essentially modern, and its long-term contribution to the emancipation of women in general is therefore considerable. In many ways its history parallels the trajectory of social reform and women's education in other communities.

A Note on Sheikh Muhammad Abdullah

The establishment of a Primary School more than a century ago, in October 1906, and its evolution into a prestigious institution of higher learning has no doubt been a monumental achievement. This achievement is, to a very great extent, the result of the indefatigable efforts of Sheikh Muhammad Abdullah (1874-1965), a pioneer of western education among Indian Muslim women in the subcontinent, and his equally dedicated wife, Wahid Jahan Begum (1886-1939). A prolific writer and a successful journalist, Sheikh Abdullah belonged to what is known as the 'Aligarh's First Generation'.

In those days, in keeping with the demands and temper of the times, Sheikh Abdullah repeatedly stressed the point that women bear the responsibility for the welfare of the family and play a crucial role in character building of their children, and must therefore, be themselves educated. 'A mother is the first teacher of the child'. He believed that the major task of education was improvement of character and, therefore, good education should lead to character building. It should promote social values of justice, liberty, and equality. He argued that value oriented education develops and nurtures moral and ethical values such as honesty, kindness, courage, dutifulness and also religious values. Value based education would enable women to distinguish between good and bad, right and wrong, proper and improper. It would engender virtues like piety, morality and humaneness along with high standards in thought and deportment.

In his autobiography, the founder explained the strict purdah that was observed as a part of school discipline. Besides, the girls were given instruction in personal hygiene and cleanliness. The College had sufficient infrastructural facilities for promoting and inculcating these habits. Sheikh Abdullah's personal opinion regarding purdah was that seclusion is like a 'silent killer'. He held that veiling as observed in India was based on custom (*rasmi purdah*) and was restrictive and more a mark of 'prestige' than of religious identity. His attitude was far ahead of his times. On crucial issues such as polygamy, Sheikh Abdullah was in broad agreement with many contemporary Muslim intellectuals. He condemned polygamy in strong terms and also said that it was not possible to treat multiple wives equally as enjoined in the Quran.

His ideas on education find similar echoes in the thoughts of other social and educational reformers of the age, like Syed Karamat Husain (1854-1917), Professor of Law and teacher of Sheikh Abdullah; Khwaja Ghulam-us-Saqlain (1850-1917), a friend and a hostel mate; and Syed Mumtaz Ali (1860-1935), an early champion of women's rights. Absorbing the ideas of great and eminent personalities of the Aligarh Movement like Khwaja Altaf Husain Hali (1837-1914), Shibli Nomani, Zakaullah, Viqarul Mulk, and Moulvi Nazir Ahmad Dehlavi (1830-1912), Sheikh Abdullah took a pragmatic approach to problems, being more of an educator than a political theorist.

Sheikh Abdullah strove hard to translate his vision and ideas of a 'new Woman' into reality. He envisioned that women who were literate and educated would prove to be better wives and companions to their husbands and better mothers and home-makers. They would better raise their children to be healthy, disciplined and good citizens of India. They would become role models for other women.

In his call for the readjustment of gender relations, Sheikh Abdullah wished that women too should become physicians, advocates, successful entrepreneurs and, above all, better human beings. Calling on them to be tolerant, accommodating, respectful of elders, and loving and affectionate to the young, he exhorted them to develop a positive attitude. Considering women to be equal partners in life, he encouraged women to develop their speaking skills by participating in the College debating club, so as to learn to be articulate and speak on issues of concern for the community and attain political representation.

Sheikh Abdullah declared:

> I would like to convey the message to the young ladies and girls of this nation that now is the time that they should be ready to shoulder the enormous responsibilities of carrying forward the torch of progress and advancement. I would like to foretell them the good news that if they would be prepared for self-help, no power, no authority would be able to deprive them from their rights. They would be equal partners in the heritage of their motherland (*Madar-i-Hind*). They would be entitled to their shares in the property inheritance and they would be co-sharers in the government services. They would be able to claim their share in all these positions, which today are the exclusive prerogative of men.

References

1. Muhammadan Anglo-Oriental Educational Conference, 1913. Report of the Female Education Section, p. 180.
2. 'Muslim Women's Education', *Comrade* edited by Muhammad Ali, 23 December 1911, No. 26, Vol. II.
3. 'Education of Muslim Girls', *Comrade*, edited by Muhammad Ali, 11 February 1911, No.5, Vol. I.
4. *Khatoon*, edited y Sheikh Abdullah, March, No. 3, Vol. 8, 1912, p. 9. This article is in the form of a repartee to Mumtaz Ali's article in *Tahzeeb Niswan* of 28th October 1911, decrying the Muslim Girls' School at Aligarh, with the objective of estranging the Muslim community from the Aligarh Muslim Girls' School. The article by Mumtaz Ali unfortunately could not be looked at due to its non-availability.

5. Muhammadan Anglo-Oriental Educational Conference, 1913. Report of the Female Education Section, p. 180.

6. Zafar ul Mulk Alvi, a journalist who edited his brother's paper, the *Al-Nazir*, a literary journal that published poems and advocated female education. A leading Khilafat agitator in Lucknow, he entered politics in 1918 with the rise of the Khilafat Movement, 1919-20, and proposed the Non-Cooperation resolution on Khilafat Day, 1st August, 1920. Cf. Francis Robinson, *Separatism Among Indian Muslims*, p. 366.

7. Muhammadan Anglo-Oriental Educational Conference, 1913. Resolution No. 2, p. 188.

8. Cora Vreede de Steurs, *Parda, A Study of Muslim Women's Life in Northern India*, p. 56.

9. Minault, Gail, 'Sheikh Abdullah, Begum Abdullah, and Sharif Education for Girls at Aligarh' in Imtiaz Ahmad (ed.) *Modernization and Social Change among Muslims in India*, Manohar Publications, 1983, p. 228.

10. Abdullah, Sheikh, *Mushahadat va Ta'asurat*, p. 240.

11. *Sawanih-Umri*, pp. 59-61.

12. Prospectus of the Muslim Girls' High School and Inter College, Aligarh, 1931-32.

13. Minault, Gail, op. cit., p. 229. See also *Khatoon*, VI, 1 January 1909, *Sawanih-Umri*, pp. 63-66.

14. Minault, Gail, op. cit., p. 229. See also *Khatoon*, VI, 1 January 1909, *Sawanih-Umri*, pp. 63-66.

15. Muhammadan Anglo-Oriental Educational Conference, 1915. Report of the Female Education Section, p. 58.

16. Ibid.

17. *Hayat-e Aftab*, p. 182.

18. *Mushahadat va Ta'ssurat*, p. 245.

19. Ibid., pp. 262-268.

20. The source used here is a copy of the Qawaid, Muslim Girls' High School and Intermediate College, 1929. But the wording and contents of the constitution of the Female Education Association clearly suggest that it was formed in 1917. This is borne out, firstly, by the

fact that Viqar ul Mulk who died in 1917 (cf. *Separation Among Indian Muslims*, p. 399) is mentioned as one of its founder members. Secondly, in the list of the founding members, with the name of Aftab Ahmad Khan, the prefix 'Honourable' indicates that it was written sometime after Aftab Ahmad Khan received appointment as Member of India Council. (Cf. *Hayat e Aftab*, pp. 224-226). Aftab Ahmad Khan received his appointment in February 1917, and joined his job as Member, India Council on 23rd September 1917.

21. Muhammadan Anglo-Oriental Educational Conference, 1915. Report of the Female Education Section, p. 146.

22. *Mushahadat va Ta'ssurat*, p. 262. There is no information as to the identity of the Board or University from which the girls appeared for the Matriculation Examination. From a communication of Sheikh Abdullah to the Vice-Chancellor, dated March 1923 (AMU Archives, File No. 53, 1922-23, Application Secy. Girls' High School for help), it becomes known that from 1923, the candidates from the School started appearing in the examination held by AMU. One may therefore, assume that till 1923 the School was sending its students for the Matriculation Examination conducted by the U.P. Board.

23. Aligarh Muslim University Archives, File No. 53, 1922-23. In the text of the letter, the school is referred to as Muslim High School, whereas in the heading it is referred to as 'Girls' High School'.

24. Aligarh Muslim University Archives, File No. 53, 1922-23. Application: Secy. Girls' High School for Help. This liberality of Begum of Bhopal is in sharp contrast with the miserly attitude of the fabulously rich Nizam who only held out a promise of 'final disposal' of the appeal made by Sheikh Abdullah on behalf of the School.

25. Aligarh Muslim University Archives, File No. 53, 1922-23.

26. Aligarh Muslim University Archives, File No. 53, 1922-23. Application: Secy. Girls' High School about Help.

27. Wilayat Husain, Mir, *Aap Biti*.

28. Aligarh Muslim University Archives, File No. 53, 1922-23. Application: Secy. Girls' High School about Help.

29. Aligarh Muslim University Archives, File No. 53, 1922-23. Request Secy. Girls' High School, re-extension date of payment loan Rs.3,500.

30. Minutes of the Special Meeting of the Executive Council, 18th January, 1925, No. 44.

31. Minutes of the Executive Council 5th July, 1926, No. 62.
32. Qawaid, Muslim Girls' High School and Intermediate College, 1929.
33. Minutes of the Executive Council, 12 May, 1929, No. 107 (15).
34. Minutes of the Executive Council, 8 June, 1929, No. 108 (17).
35. Muhammadan Anglo-Oriental Educational Conference, 1933, p. 49.
36. Prospectus of the Muslim Girls' High School and Intermediate College, Aligarh, 1931-32.
37. Muhammadan Anglo-Oriental Educational Conference, 1934.
38. Muhammadan Anglo-Oriental Educational Conference, 1936. Resolution No. 4, p. 74.
39. Muhammadan Anglo-Oriental Educational Conference, 1937. Resolution No. 1, p. 31.
40 Muhammadan Anglo-Oriental Educational Conference, 1937, p. 36.
41. Minutes of the Executive Council, 17 July 1938, No. 241(11a).
42. Ibid.
43. Minutes of the Executive Council, 25 September, 1938, No. 243, 30 (5b iii).
44. Minutes of the Executive Council, 18 December, 1938, No. 246 (47b).
45. Mohammadan Anglo-Oriental Educational Conference, 1938, p. 38.
46. First Meeting of the Women's College Managing Committee held on 30th November, 1942. Report given in the Minutes of the Executive Council, 1942.
47. Recommendations of the Managing Committee of the Women's College, at its meeting held on 22 August 1943, made to the Executive Council as given in Minutes of the Executive Council, 1943.
48. First meeting of the Managing Committee of the Women's College held on 30 November 1942 as given in the Minutes of the Executive Council, 1942.
49. *Aligarh Institute Gazette*, Vol. 43, No. 12, December, 2006.
50. Ibid.
51. Ibid.

Chapter VIII

Establishment of Schools by Other Indigenous Efforts

In the second half of the nineteenth century isolated efforts were made for the education of Muslim women. In the United Provinces, it was only with the activism of Sheikh Abdullah in the late nineteenth century, that a serious and sustained effort began which provided the much-needed fillip to Muslim women's education. However, it was no mean task to carry forward a campaign that had few supporters and many adversaries. The dogged perseverance of Sheikh Abdullah against all opposition and the fact that Begum Abdullah and other eminent ladies like the Begum of Bhopal were fully involved in the movement helped the movement for women's education to grow. In due course, the movement for the education of Muslim women became a part of the wider Aligarh Movement and there was no looking back.

Influenced probably by the reformist tendencies within a section of the Aligarh Movement, similar movements for the education of Muslim women took roots in towns like Agra, Rampur, Allahabad and Lucknow. They faced the same kind of opposition and challenges as in Aligarh. In Agra, Saeed Ahmad Marharwi, the founder of the Saghir Fatima Intermediate College for Muslim girls mobilized the women themselves, who were most supportive and forthcoming with help and donations to start a school for Muslim girls. The foundation laid by Saeed Ahmad Marharwi proved to be strong enough for his supporters to carry forward the work even after his death. In Rampur, the State took upon itself to initiate and promote Muslim women's education. Though finance was not a problem, efforts made for educating Muslim girls by the State faced the same narrow-minded bigotry, as did Sheikh Abdullah's or even Karamat Husain's efforts for the same. In Allahabad, it was mainly an industrial house that became the mainstay for the education of Muslim girls. Though the Hamidia Girls' Degree College, Allahabad, was founded and established by Begum Khursheed Khwaja, daughter of a former Chief Justice of Allahabad, it was sustained and nurtured by the selfless dedication and commitment of the ladies of the Shervani family and their well wishers. The Hamidia College was established notwithstanding the constraints of space and finance. Likewise, progressive Muslim men and educated Muslim ladies of the time sustained its progress with great dedication and commitment. In Lucknow, the Taleemgah-e-Niswan was established by Begum Inam Habibullah, an educated lady from an eminent and progressive family. In a way, it was purely a family effort. Moulvi Karamat Husain, a visionary and a torchbearer, like his student Sheikh Abdullah, established a school in Lucknow, which later came to be known as the Karamat Husain Muslim Girls' P. G. College. Under his able stewardship and with generous help from the Raja of Mahmudabad, the school progressed. Unfortunately Karamat Husain died within five years of founding the school and there was no one in his family (he was a widower and survived his only issue, a daughter) to take up his mantle and push the school to greater heights. The Raja stood steadfast in his resolve to help the school and he continued his support to the school as long as he lived.

Thus, in the United Provinces the idea of Muslim Women's education took root in an environment of general opposition. It was the foresight, grit and determination of a few individuals that saw the establishment of exclusive schools for Muslim girls. Once this was done, it did not take long for the community to realize the need and importance of education for girls.

Karamat Husain and the Muslim Girls' P.G. College, Lucknow

Justice Syed Karamat Husain (1854-1917), founder of the Muslim Girls' P.G. College, Lucknow that bears his name, belonged to a family of Service Gentry who had served the Nawabs of Awadh as teachers and religious functionaries.[1] The school established by him in 1912 was named after its founder on his death and 'remains a monument to his memory'.[2]

Karamat Husain belonged to a family who were saiyids and shi'as with a tradition of Islamic learning. Karamat Husain's grandfather, Mufti Syed Mohammad Quli Khan, was learned in Islamic Law. His father, Moulvi Syed Siraj Husain, was not only educated in the classical languages Arabic and Persian and in Islamic sciences, but was also a scholar of Mathematics. He was the first man in the family to learn English. He served as a sub-judge in the British administration and was later employed in Bundelkhand.[3]

Karamat Husain was thus prepared by his family heritage to enter into the legal and administrative service of the British or of some indirectly administered princely state. But the circumstances of his life were different and these influenced him later in life. His mother died when he was five or six, his father when he was eleven. Hence he was orphaned as a child. Of a shy nature, he derived comfort from such books as *Najhul Baligha* (the maxims of Ali) in Arabic and the *Anwar-i-Suhali* (animal fables) in Persian.[4]

His paternal uncle, Syed Hamid Husain, a learned *mujtahid*, became his guardian in 1865. He took him to Lucknow to continue his Islamic education. He accompanied his uncle on a Hajj pilgrimage, which was Karamat Husain's first contact with the outside world. This exposure to the outside world only increased his desire to study further.[5] Being an intelligent and a quick learner, he continued his education in Lucknow. Karamat Husian mastered the Islamic curriculum, classical languages and *fiqh*.[6]

Karamat Husain married the granddaughter of one of his teachers, Sultanul Ulama Syed Muhammad, and had a daughter by the marriage. His wife died young and he never remarried.[7] He also lost his elder brother and his only daughter too.[8] Gail Minault appropriately feels that it was natural that 'such a scholarly, lonely man would have taken up the cause of women's education at a time when others were still opposed to it. His independence of mind and his firm grounding in the Islamic scriptures perhaps gave him the courage to do what was right and not worry about unfavourable public opinion'.[9]

After leaving Lucknow in 1874, Karamat Husain obtained a job as Head Moulvi in Raj Kumar College, a school founded by Dr. Stratton, the Political Agent for Bundelkhand, for the sons of the princes of the region. For this position, he needed no English. He worked hard at studying English and obtained a fair degree of fluency in the language within two years. He then studied western science and philosophy, hungry for books by Darwin, Huxley, Spencer and Mill.[10]

After completing a stint of three years at Raj Kumar College, Karamat Husain was appointed Mir Munshi to the Political Agent, Stratton, where he earned a reputation for efficiency and incorruptibility.[11] Stratton then appointed him to the post of Diwan of the state of Narsinghgarh, whose ruler agreed to pay for his studies in Law, though Karamat Husain's personal choice was to study Medicine and become a doctor so that he could help people and save lives. So in 1886, at the age of 32, Karamat Husain accompanied the Raja to England to study for the Bar at Middle Temple. He became Barrister-at-Law in early 1889 and returned to India only to hear of the death of his elder brother. He established his barrister's practice in Allahabad.[12]

Karamat Husain's first contact with a society in which women played an accepted social role was in England. He, together with a number of his contemporaries, formed the Anjuman-i-Ta'lim un-Niswan (Association for Women's Education), but the Association in London never really took off the ground. It was premature to form the Association in London, for the real work had to be done here in India.[13] While in London, Karamat Husain realized that the progress of a nation depended on the education of its women. He came back to India in July 1889 and in November 1890 he began his practice in the Allahabad High Court as a Barrister. It was here that his ideas and his commitment to women's education crystallized and took form.

The suggestion by him to introduce the subject of women's education on the platform of the Muhammadan Educational Conference to be held in Allahabad in 1890 quite shocked the leading members of the Conference, but Karamat Husain was undaunted.

Karamat Husain joined M.A.O. College as its first Professor of Law in 1891.[14] His appointment was approved by Sir Syed Ahmad Khan, notwithstanding his reputation as a supporter of female education. Karamat Husain became a member of the Muslim Educational Conference in 1891, and when the Conference met in Aligarh in the same year Karamat Husain proposed a resolution, which was adopted by the Conference.

The resolution reads as follows:

> The Conference feels that according to the conditions prevailing, Muslims should work for the education of women side by side with the men, since the advancement of the community depends on this. The education should be such that it advances the religious, literary and cultural life of women, so that with their education the future generations would stand to gain.[15]

Nothing thereafter was done for female education and Karamat Husain resigned his professorship and came back to Allahabad where he resumed his practice at the High Court and simultaneously taught Law at the Muir Central College.[16] In Allahabad, he succumbed to the desire to do something concrete for female education and so with a few like minded people, of both communities – "members of the growing Indian middle class"[17] – he raised a fund to start a girls' school. In 1890, a girls' school was established named after Sir Charles Crosthwaite, the Lt. Governor of U.P., since he had extended the much needed helping hand. Known to be a crusader for female education, Karamat Husain was selected in 1904 to be a member of the Committee of Indian gentlemen to advise the government of the United Provinces as to the methods of advancing female education that were practicable under the then existing conditions.[18]

While still at Allahabad Karamat Husain became a judge of the Allahabad High Court and remained so from January 1908 until June 1912. During his tenure as judge, Karamat Husain made original contributions to clarifying the most confusing aspects of Muslim Law. In recognition of his services, Allahabad University appointed him a fellow. Dr. Athar Abbas Rizvi in his book *Socio-Cultural History of Isna' Ashari Shi'is of India* writes that from a *mujtahid* and an administrator of petty states, Syed Karamat Husain rose to the position of a barrister and a judge. He elevates Karamat Husain to the rank of Sir Syed Ahmed Khan since he was successful in promoting female education in the midst of hysterical opposition.[19] On retiring from this post for reasons of health, Karamat Husain devoted himself solely to his commitment to female education. He went on to establish a Muslim Girls' School in Lucknow in 1912. In this endeavour, invaluable help, support and encouragement was rendered by the Raja of Mahmudabad, Sir Muhammad Ali Muhammad, a leading Taluqdar of Awadh.[20]

Both, the Raja and Syed Karamat Husain, worked together on this mammoth task. The question of funds was tackled first. Karamat Husain contributed the proceeds of the income of his land, to the tune of one lakh twenty-five thousand rupees, which he set up as *waqf* and the Raja assigned the revenues of several villages amounting to Rupees 600 per month to the school.[21]

Justice Karamat Husain was no doubt a great champion of female education. It will be interesting to note here how he countered the opposition of fellow Muslim professionals. Steeped in conservatism, one of them warned him that God would 'blacken his face' if he went ahead with his agenda of Muslim female education. Karamat Husain replied that it would not make much of a difference since he already enjoyed a dark complexion. To another opponent he said that he would prefer to be cursed and Muslim women educated than he retain his good name and Muslim women remain in ignorance.[22]

His stand on Muslim women's education can be gleaned from his speech on the occasion of a meeting of the Anjuman i-ala-Talim Niswan (Association for the Higher Education of Indian Women) held in Allahabad in December 1915, in which he argued that if men want future generations to succeed, it is imperative that they educate their daughters.

Karamat Husain began his speech by saying that in India the division of labour starts at home. While men have to earn, women have to manage the home. In managing the home, a number of tasks have to be done like managing accounts, managing the limited income economically, keeping the house clean and comfortable, and creating a healthy environment. Besides, the house has to be organised and kept in order. Cooking nutritious food, arranging for comfortable clothing, and tending the sick, besides managing all expenditure within the income, was all part of a woman's duty towards her family members. The birth of children would add further to her duties. The woman is responsible for their health, cleanliness, social and moral/religious upbringing, so as to enable them to live in this world with good health, ease and respect. This, he says, is the more important job. The men had just to help and support the womenfolk.

Furthering his argument, Karamat Husain said that for a child to be good, it is necessary for the women to be good, for the child, who is a part of the mother, would reflect her qualities. The mother tends the child in his/her tender years. This upbringing produces the qualities of the mother in the child. If the mother is not conversant with the proper ways of bringing up a child, the child will be spoilt.

A woman is not born with the required qualities necessary to manage a home. Such capabilities had to be acquired through education and training. It is incumbent on us to give our girls the kind of education and training that will make them capable of discharging their household duties well, if we want our future generation to live a life of good health, ease and respect. Education dispels the evil and darkness in a woman's mind rather than creating it. One must be convinced about the need for education and then try to convince others and make it a mass movement. Keeping women uneducated should be thought of as a great sin and a drawback. After being convinced as to the need of educating women, people with true intention and desire to promote the cause should come forward with help in setting up madrasas for women. He outlined the curriculum that should be taught in the girls' madrasas to include:

- Reading and writing so that one can acquire all the knowledge that is available in the world.
- Arithmetic which is necessary to keep track of income and expenditure.
- Health which is very necessary.
- Hygiene and cleanliness to keep the body and mind healthy.
- Exercise to enable them to spend time in the open.

Education is necessary for a healthy mind and body, he said, and not only for getting jobs. Those who feel that girls can be educated at home and that madrasas are unnecessary were wrong, according to him. Sending girls to schools was much better because the girls would get access to better teachers and a broader curriculum than in any home education. A good madrasa does not adversely affect behaviour as was presumed, he argued, whereas the opposite was true. In a good madrasa, physical, mental and behavioural health is taken care of. The superstitions and useless customs that had crept into the culture would disappear with proper education and enlightenment. They would be better human beings, better Muslims, mothers, wives and guides to their children, if they learnt properly about their religion and its requirements.

Those who feel that women will compete with men after being educated have a defeatist attitude, he said. Men should respond with more courage, since except for some physical differences, men and women are made equals. Another necessity for education of women is that, the men now educated would demand educated wives.

In conclusion, he declared that those who contribute to women remaining uneducated, are sinning in the eyes of Allah and of the human race and are spoiling and destroying the future generation. If the women of any community are backward, men of that community can never advance.[23]

The school was founded in November 1912 in rented accommodation in the city[24] with a boarding house ensuring seclusion. A boarding school, it was felt, would provide residential facility for Muslim girls as it was neither safe nor permissible at that time for young girls to travel long distances in search of academics. To do away with this handicap, initially a humble beginning was made with just six beds.

The Raja of Mahmudabad had arranged the house of Chowdhry Nusrat Ali Sandile, a Talukdar. Later it had to move from Qaiser-bagh to Nisar Saheb's house (Kothi) in 18, Outram House, since some unscrupulous elements had started defaming the school, sending 'riff raffs' who sang theatre ghazals standing beneath the school building.[25] In 1920, it moved again to a building in the suburbs of Lucknow, that had originally been the Government Girls' High School, built on land donated by the Raja of Mahmudabad.[26] Today, it stands there in the stature of a Post-graduate institution for girls, realizing the dreams of Justice Syed Karamat Husain for women's education. The College presently imparts education to approximately 7000 girls in its three wings.

The School had its first Principal in Miss Amna Ethel Pope. An English woman, she had converted to Islam and had come in 1910 to superintend the boarding house at Crosthwaite. The speech which the Principal, Miss Pope, gave on the Founding Day of the School echoes the same sentiments as that of the proponents of Muslim female education. She stated in her inaugural speech that no community could prosper until the women of that community were educated. Miss Pope also assured the mothers of the girls that she would carefully follow the rules for veiling and would promote Muslim religious worship and ethical and social ideals. Regular Namaz and the observance of fast would be compulsory. Urdu, Persian, Arabic and English would be taught together with cooking and home-science. Stitching, cooking, embroidery and handicrafts would be included. Hygiene and health education and their strict observance would also be a part of their education. They would be groomed to be polite, well-behaved and dutiful daughters who after marriage would be able to become loving wives, good mothers and efficient managers of their homes.[27]

Lady Meston, wife of the Lt. Governor, inaugurated the School officially in March 1913. In her speech, she emphasized the need to train mothers for the betterment of future generations.[28]

Qurratulain Haider, in her book *Kar-e-Jahan Daraz Hai* names students who got admitted in the first year. They were as follows:

1. Qurratulain Haider, the illustrious Urdu novelist herself
2. Someone known to the writer as Button Baji
3. Jannat, Chowdhry Nabiullah's daughter
4. Sakina, Justice Karamat Husain's granddaughter
5. Kishwar, Justice Samiullah Beg's daughter
6. Hajra, daughter of Raza Ali, Qurratulain Haider's paternal uncle.

Four daughters of Chowdhry Muhammad Ali Rudaulvi, Kajjan, Allan, Huma and Chabban, were admitted to the boarding house. Later Shammoo, daughter of Nawab Saheb Janjira of Bombay, was also admitted. Among these girls, Jannat and Button Baji were day scholars. Jannat came to school in a phaeton with her grandmother as escort. Button Baji came with the *kahar*s and *khidmatgar*s sitting on a *chowpehla*.[29]

Initially, on opening of the boarding house, for about 8-10 days, food for the boarders came from the Raja of Mahmudabad's kitchen. Later an independent kitchen was established for the boarding house. Karamat Husain personally bore the expenses of the boarding house. Only the tuition fee was taken from the students. In 1916, the school had 50 girl students.[30] During the inaugural function, the girls read Maulana Safi's poem which he had written for the occasion.[31]

By 1915, the strength of the Muslim Girls' School in Lucknow was twenty-four, of whom seventeen were boarders. In the same year, a grant of Rs.1200 per year was given by the Begum of Bhopal, when she visited the school. This provided to some extent the much needed financial stability and security. By 1923, the total number of students had risen to fifty-two.[32]

Over the years, the strength of the school increased manifold, and in 1924 it became a High School. It rose to the status of an Inter College in 1936, and eventually to a Degree College in 1946. In the year 2000, Post graduate classes were opened in English, B.Sc classes were introduced in 2002 and B.Ed. in 2005.

Syed Karamat Husain had died on the 19 th of April, 1917, remaining active in the field of girls education till the very end. Patronage of the Raja of Mahmudabad did not cease and he named the school after its founder.[33]

Syed Karamat Husain wrote books and articles on Muslim law and Arabic philosophy. He played an active role in defending the cause of Urdu. His name figures as a signatory on the address that[34] eminent Indian Muslims presented to the Viceroy at Shimla in 1906. He was a member of the Provincial Committee of the All India Muslim League elected at Dacca in 1906 and supported the agitation for separate Muslim electorates.[35]

Gail Minault in 'Syed Karamat Husain and Education for Women' aptly sums up his contribution:

> Syed Karamat Husain, jurist, scholar and a crusader for women's education, lived a lonely life and fought a lonely battle. A combination of traditional and modern learning, and intellectual acceptance by religious scholars, western educated Indians and British administration alike, led Karamat Husain to high judicial office, but also enabled him to champion an unpopular cause and give it the prestige of his concern and patronage. Today, his ideas may not seem revolutionary or even particularly innovative... But Karamat Husain's single minded courage and devotion to the cause, his unspectacular but solid achievements, deserve respect... He quietly inspired three major women's educational institutions in U.P.: in Allahabad, Aligarh and Lucknow. The latter bears his name. It is an appropriate memorial.[36]

Although the institution was started with the primary object of advancing the cause of education among Muslim girls, its portals have always been open to the students belonging to all communities without any distinction of caste and creed. A recognized minority institution, its purpose is to impart quality education to women of all faiths and communities, more precisely the minorities and weaker sections, and to provide an environment and facilities for the all round development of their personalities.

The stated goals and objectives of the College are:[37]

- To promote and provide opportunities for academic excellence by developing critical thinkers and adding new perspectives to the world of knowledge.
- To promote students' integrated spiritual, moral, cultural and physical development.
- To instill confidence and a sense of self-reliance and self-esteem among the students.
- To develop an ability to use knowledge to transform lives.
- To empower students by preparing them for the challenges and complexities of life in the twenty-first century based on value system.

Hamidia Girls' Intermediate College, Allahabad

During the early 20th century, when schools were being established both for Muslim boys and girls as a result of the efforts made by the All India Educational Conference and Muslim girls' schools had already been established in Aligarh and Lucknow, it was ironical that in Allahabad, despite its being a centre of education, having a university, a large Muslim population and a large number of Muslim advocates, barristers, judges and government officials, there was no educational institution for the education of their daughters. Begum Khursheed Khwaja,[38] daughter of the ex-Chief Justice of the Nizam of Hyderabad, filled this need of a girls' school in Allahabad. Motivated by her father and her desire to protect and maintain the religious and cultural identity of the Muslim community, and fired by her zeal to emancipate Muslim girls from 'gloom, darkness and illiteracy', Begum Khursheed Khwaja opened a primary school for Muslim girls in Dr. Syed Ali Zaidi's house in the narrow lane of Pathargali, Shahganj, on the 4th of May, 1932, in memory of her father, late Nawab Sir Buland Jung Hamidullah Khan, former Chief Justice of Hyderabad. This school came to be known as Hamidia Girls' Primary School.

The beginning was very humble, a few girls and two amateur teachers. All expenses of the school were borne by the Begum herself. Her efforts bore fruit and very soon a Management Committee was established under the purview of the Association for the Education of Muslim Women of Allahabad (Anjuman Taalimat-e-Muslim Khawateen).[39]

Begum Khursheed Khwaja became the Managing Committee's Honorary Secretary. The Begum then started on a mission to enlist the sympathy, active support and patronage of top influential personalities and the elite of the city for the infant school. The Society had the good fortune of having a distinguished personality, Hon'ble Sir Shah Muhammad Sulaiman, the Chief Justice of Allahabad High Court, as its first President. Other distinguished patrons involved with the school were:

1. Begum Niamatullah Sahiba, w/o Hon'ble Justice Niamatulla, Allahabad
2. Mrs. P.N. Sapru, daughter-in-law of a leading lawyer of Allahabad High Court and a great lover of Urdu literature
3. Begum Iqbal, wife of Justice Sir Iqbal Ahmad, Allahabad
4. Begum Ghaznafrullah, wife of Hafiz Muhammad, a distinguished businessman of Allahabad
5. Begum Hashmat Ali, wife of Mr. Hashmat Ali an administrative officer of that time
6. Begum Haji Mohammad Hussain
7. Begum Sayeed Jahan Shervani
8. Begum Khan Bahadur.

With such high profile patronage and support, the school was put on the road of progress and it soon forged ahead.[40]

Although the object of the institution was to impart education, including higher education to Muslim women, in keeping with their linguistic and ideological development, its portals remained open to all, regardless of religious affiliation.[41]

The first Principal was Miss D. Bewen who held the post from July 1932 to July 1935. Ms. Shamsus Zoha Zaidi and Mrs. Madholal took great pains to teach the girls, bearing all expenses themselves. Due to Begum Khursheed Khwaja's untiring and selfless service, the School was upgraded to a high school in 1946 and became affiliated to the Board of High School and Intermediate Education, and was hence known as Hamidia Girls' High School.[42]

Begum Mahmood Jahan, wife of Haji Syed Mohammad Husain, Bar-at-law, became the President of the Management Committee. On Begum Khursheed Khwaja's request, Begum Haji Mohammad Husain gave her house in Pathargali at a monthly rent of Rs.200 to the Hamidia School. This solved the problem of space and building.

At some time during this period, Begum Khursheed Khwaja left for Aligarh with her husband Abdul Majeed, Bar at Law, and entrusted the entire management of the School to the Managing Committee under the overall supervision of the registered body i.e., Anjuman Taalimat Muslim Khawateen, Allahabad.[43]

In 1951, Syed Wahidul Hasan, Registrar, Education Department, Uttar Pradesh, on retirement, became Manager and Secretary of the Hamidia High School. He had the required experience and was instrumental in getting the High School upgraded to Intermediate level for arts subjects only. The School now came to be known as Hamidia Girls' Intermediate College. He remained the Manager for fifteen years. In this period he introduced science, tailoring and home science at the High School and Intermediate level. The strength of the school rose to 3,500 students.

When the problem of space and infrastructure became acute, Begum Haji Mohammad Hussain gave away the property as *wakf* to Hamidia Girls' College with the following conditions:

- That during her life she would be given the rent of the building

- On her demise, the masjid Kotwal Saheb, Pathargali, adjacent to the building, was to be maintained and expenses borne by the College
- Maintenance and upkeep of the family burial ground situated in Kaledanda, Himmatganj, must continue to be undertaken by the College
- The College would arrange for Qurbani every year on behalf of Haji Liaquat Husain, kotwal, his son, Haji Mohammad Husain, and wife Begum Mohammad Husain.

On agreeing to the above conditions, the Hamidia Girls' Intermediate College, got its own building. The Intermediate College is running in two shifts. The first shift is for primary classes and the second for High School and Intermediate classes.[44]

Syed Wahidul Hasan died in 1966 and in his place Syed Asadullah Kazmi, Director of Training Colleges, Uttar Pradesh (Retd.) became Manager. He was a competent and experienced man in the field of education. Humaira Nikhat was selected for the post of Principal and remained in the post for a long time. Begum Akhtar Ajmal Khan, daughter of the founder of the College, Begum Khursheed Khwaja, and wife of Mr. Ajmal Khan, a noted doctor and Chief Medical Officer, Allahabad, succeeded Syed Asadullah Kazmi as Manager in 1969.The President, Begum Mohammad Husain, also died at the same time. In her place, Begum T.R. Shervani,[45] wife of Mr. Mustafa Rashid Shervani, a noted industrialist running Geep Industry, Allahabad, became the President. Begum A.A. Khan and Begum T.R. Shervani were close relatives. The Intermediate College progressed under their stewardship. The members of the Managing Committee were as follows:

1. Mustafa Rashid Shervani
2. Nafees Ahmad Kazmi, Advocate
3. Zulfiqarullah
4. Syed Bashir Ahmad, Advocate

5. Riazuddin, Principal, Majidah Islamia College
6. Begum Ahsanullah
7. M. Sadiq Husain, Principal, Mustafa Rashid Shervani Intermedi ate College.

The Principal, Mrs. Humaira Nikhat, proved to be a very efficient and competent person and was able to elicit the cooperation and help of the Staff Members. She also had good relations with the Education Department of the government and the Management Committee of the College, due to which the College did not face any adverse situation or circumstance.

Mrs. Humaira Nikhat also obtained permission for introducing science subjects from the Board of High School and Intermediate Education, Uttar Pradesh. The senior science teacher, Mrs. Laeeq Bano, also helped the Principal through her own contacts to get the permission for science classes. But due to lack of laboratories in the school, there was delay in starting the science classes. Their efforts finally bore fruit and a grant of $1 lakh was given for the laboratories by the Islamic Development Bank of Jeddah, with the stipulation that a consultant engineer be appointed for the supervision of the building, and this task was very well performed by one of the members of the Committee, Mr. Mohammad Ahsanullah, an engineer by profession.[46]

With the distinct success of the Intermediate College, the demand for higher education grew among the families of Muslim girls who had cleared the Higher Secondary course. The Manager, Mrs. A.A. Khan, initiated the efforts to make this Intermediate College into a Degree College. The Principal of the College also played a commendable role in making this effort a success. To meet the demand, a Degree College was provisionally started in 1975 in a small corner of the crowded Intermediate College.[47] Enrolment in the Degree College increased and the space available became inadequate to accommodate them. Mr. M.R. Shervani and

Begum T. R. Shervani wholeheartedly extended financial support to the School.[48] A relative of Begum T.R. Shervani, who held a high position in the B.C.C.I. Bank, London, was able to arrange a donation of Rupees three lakhs from the Bank. Along with Begum A.A. Khan, Begum Tazeen Ahsanullah was also helpful in getting the College established. Luckily, Sri Hemvati Nandan Bahuguna was the Chief Minister of Uttar Pradesh at that time. Begum A.A. Khan's eldest son, Dr. Mansoor Hasan,[49] enjoyed good rapport with the Chief Minister. On his recommendation, the Chief Minister gave an endowment of Rs.55,000 from his discretionary fund and obtained permission for starting the Degree College in 1975. The foundation stone of the Degree College was laid by Hazrat Maulana Syed Abul Hasan Ali Nadvi on November 7, 1982. The U.G.C. did not give any grant for 5 years. The Staff worked on low salaries. Begum Tazeen Ahsanullah agreed to work as Honorary Principal of the Degree College. The foundation of the Hamidia Degree College was laid in an area called Sultanpur Bhawa on Noorullah Road in Allahabad. It is now affiliated to Allahabad University. Begum Tazeen Ahsanullah is the present Manager and Dr. Rehana Tariq is the Principal. Apart from the Arts Faculty, the College has permission for B.Ed classes also. Begum A.A. Khan's brother, Mr. Ajmal Khwaja, has donated a sum of Rs.16 lakhs for the purchase of land. Mr. Noorullah Khan who resides in Florida, Orlando, U.S.A. has assured that he would get the building of the B.Ed. classes constructed from his own resources.

In 1975, Mrs. T.R. Shervani and Mrs. A.A. Khan appointed Mr. Saghir Ahmad Siddiqui, District Inspector of Schools, (Retd.) as Manager and Secretary of the Degree Section, and Mr. Sadiq was appointed as the Joint Secretary. Likewise from 1976, Mrs. T.R. Shervani was President, Mrs. A.A. Khan, Vice-President and Mr. Saghir Ahmad was Manager cum Secretary of the Degree College.

On the demise of Mr.Saghir Ahmad Siddiqui in 1995, the post of Manager cum Secretary of the Degree Section was entrusted to Mr. Sadiq Husain, and Mr. Tahir Husain became the Joint Secretary. Mr. M.Z. Khan and Mr. Saleem Iqbal Shervani became members of the Managing Committee.

In 1998, the President Mrs. T.R. Shervani entrusted the post of President to her sister, Begum Rashida Khan. Begum A.A. Khan also retired, sold her property in Allahabad and shifted to Lucknow. Dr. Shakira Qazmi became Vice-President and Dr. Imama Khatoon Rizvi became second Vice-President.

The Principal of the Intermediate College, Ms. Humaira Nikhat retired after six years of active service and Dr. Abida Hasan, the senior teacher of the Intermediate College, took over as officiating Principal for a year.

In July 2000, Ms. Khairunissa Sabir was selected as the Principal of the Intermediate Section and worked in that post for two years. During her tenure, permission was granted to introduce computers at School and Intermediate level. Ms. Laeeqa Bano, lecturer, helped a lot in introducing computers to the school. An ex-member of Parliament contributed a sum of 71 lakhs for the purchase of computers.

On Mrs. K.N. Sabir's retirement in 2001, the present Principal of the Intermediate Section, Ms Shamim Bano was appointed and has been working in that post from July 2002. She has focused her attention in improving the infrastructure of the Intermediate College. Besides having helped in the opening of nursery classes, she has also been responsible in improving the overall result of the school in the Board examinations.

At present [2007-2008] the School has 28 sections of Primary classes, 18 sections of Junior High School, 10 sections of High School and 8 sections of Intermediate classes. The total strength of the School is now more than 3,500 girls.

At present the strength of the Degree College is about 2000 students, out of which about 90% come from underprivileged Muslim minority class. The College states its aim as that of providing opportunities and a platform for their growth and development. It is getting the desired results by introducing IT and other vocational courses. It is striving to maintain high academic standards and provides a set of well-qualified students capable of contributing positively towards national development, a prerogative they would not have enjoyed had they remained deprived of opportunities.[50]

The Degree College, under the Principalship of Dr. Rehana Tariq and Manager Mrs. Tazeen Ahsanullah is pursuing the task of imparting higher education along with professional and technical training, and new subjects and schemes are being introduced in the College. The College has two faculties, Arts and Commerce, six Vocational subjects, two at the Degree level, Office Management and Secretarial Practices (OFF), Computer Application in Social Sciences (CAS), and three Certificate/Diploma Courses (i) Fashion Designing and Kashidakari (ii) Urdu Journalism and Mass Communication (iii) Translation proficiency in Arabic and (iv) Two years Diploma in Urdu Kitabat sanctioned by Urdu Academy, Lucknow for ten selected students free of cost.[51]

Teaching is carried out by a team of twenty-two well-qualified Staff. To encourage toppers, the College facilitates them with medals and scholarships. Remedial coaching classes (under UGC scheme) are being conducted for those students who are not able to perform well. A Minority Coaching Centre (sponsored by the UGC) has been set up which provides coaching to minority students for different competitive examinations like U.D.C., L.D.C., Railway, Bank exams, B.Ed entrance test, since 1988. Seven N.S.S. units are also functioning.[52]

Scholarships for OBC, SC/ST, BPL students and financial assistance for *bidi* workers' wards are also arranged by the College. To provide healthy and wholesome experience to its students, the

College maintains a canteen and provides purified water. A qualified doctor is attached to the College for first aid and emergency.

Workshops and seminars are a regular practice to groom students intellectually. The College magazine *Kavish* is published every year, which provides a platform for creative writing and motivates budding writers. Students are encouraged to participate in extra-curricular activities so that they develop into responsible citizens.[53] The College can boast of being the first college in Allahabad and the third in U.P. to get itself accredited by NAAC in 2002 and achieve 'B' grade.

This College is a perfect example of an institution being run in harmony by a team of office bearers whose diligence and selfless service and dedication has enabled the College to attain many of its goals. This minority institution is 'committed to the progress and empowerment of womenfolk and nurtures the vision of serving the nation'.

Taleemgah-e-Niswan, Lucknow

The Taleemgah-e-Niswan, an Intermediate College, is a government aided minority institution for Muslim girls. Situated in Jagat Narain Road of Lucknow, a Muslim populated area, it has approximately 2,500 Muslims girls on its rolls. It neither possesses its own building nor does the land on which it stands is owned by it. The building belongs to Anjuman Islah Muslameen and the land is the property of the Sunni Wakf Board.[54] Established in 1929, as a small *Maktab* by Begum Inam Habibullah,[55] her sister Rafia Fasahat Husain, and her relative, Jamila, in a rented building it later grew to become an Intermediate College.[56]

Although the Begum was not formally educated at school, she was taught to read and write Urdu and Hindi and a bit of English at home.[57] A social activist, the education of Muslim girls was an issue dear to her heart. The one fear she had from the very onset was that deprivation of Muslim girls from education would keep the society backward, especially as they could not go to schools because they observed strict purdah.[58] She also knew that parents would not allow girls to go out of their homes and least of all to schools unless there were arrangements for strict seclusion or purdah. The Muslim girls did not attend other government or missionary schools as their parents did not allow them to attend such schools, where there were no arrangements for their security and seclusion or were said to be converting their students to Christianity. So a school was necessary, which, besides being affordable, would provide religious education and have proper arrangements for security and purdah. Moreover, since the poor Muslim families were mostly vegetable hawkers, living in the Aminabad and Chowk areas of Lucknow, such a school close to their homes was required. The girls could get some time to study only after completing their household chores and looking after their younger siblings. They could not afford to pay for conveyance, nor had they the time or permission to travel long distances to attend schools opened either through government or private enterprise. As compared to them, the non-Muslim girls did not suffer from these constraints, as they were free to attend any school, purdah being a non-issue with them. So the Begum took it upon herself to establish a school for the poor Muslim girls of the area that would cater to their needs. The Begum was able to attract the girls, and the school thus established in 1929, on Jagat Narain Road in Lucknow came to be known as Taleemgah-e-Niswan.[59] Keeping in mind the tradition of strict purdah, the school had all women staff and workers. The driving force behind the school was of course Begum Inam Habibullah herself.[60] The school started as a *Maktab* for the poor purdah observing Muslim girls where they would get religious education together with lessons of 'good behaviour and decency' considered to be a hallmark of every good and decent

Muslim woman. English and other subjects were also introduced later.[61]

Funds are necessary for the growth and development of every school and the case of Taleemgah-e-Niswan was no exception. Though the school caters to poor Muslim girls, the Muslim community by and large has not shown much sensitivity and has not encouraged the school to grow and prosper. With a few exceptions, the Muslim community has not come forward with much help.[62] The lack of interest and apathy shown by the Muslim community is to a large extent responsible for the run down, dilapidated condition of the building and lack of resources for its students.[63] Some parts of the building need urgent repair. The Manager, Mr. Shakir Ali Siddiqui, in the Annual Report reiterates emphatically that the institution has not been able to develop due to the indifference of the Muslim community, nor is it sustained by their help.[64]

The institution does not have a building of its own even today. The school that was started in an old rented building 70 years ago, and is now an Intermediate College, still exists on rented premises. This is a sad reflection on the Muslim community, and as much on the Government. Lack of infrastructural facilities also meant that the school authorities had to face insurmountable difficulties to get the school recognized. Facilities like sports and new subjects cannot be provided to the students even though there is ample demand for them. Despite the lack of space, this institution attracts girls for admission, and very year about 700-800 girls are refused admission. The present building belongs to Anjuman Islah Muslameen.[65]

A few sympathetic members of the Muslim community did extend financial help and as a result 3 rooms were repaired. People who have extended financial help are:

1. The President of the Managing Committee, Begum Hamida Habibullah

2. Begum Khwaja Nooruddin Sahiba, Member, Managing Committee
3. Mrs. Shahina Hasan, Principal and other Staff Members
4. Parents and Teachers' Association's contribution
5. An anonymous donor contributed Rs.20, 000 under promise of anonymity.

The family of Ahmad Husain Dildar Husain, Tambakuwale, especially Begum Asghar Husain, finds special mention from Begum Hamida Habibullah and are included among the large hearted people who have encouraged and helped the school financially.[66]

The Begum of Bhopal surprisingly did not extend any monetary help. She came to visit the school, extended her verbal encouragement and was delighted to see the place. Some NRIs have extended considerable financial support to the school, not wanting their names to be publicised.[67] The people who have extended help, support and encouragement in recent times are the Managing Committee members, specially the ex-Manager, Mr. Shakir Ali, the present Manager, Mr. Abdul Razzak, and the present Principal of the school, Mrs. Shahina Hasan.[68] The school has not been able to attain the honour of an institution of higher learning because of certain constraints, although efforts are still on.

However, it must be said that the Taleemgah-e-Niswan has in a way been able to achieve its aim, that of providing affordable education to poor Muslim girls and making them economically independent, so that they are able to cope with the pressures and challenges of the modern world. Most of the girls are employed by SEWA (Self-Employed Women's Association) in the *chikan* embroidery business, instituted with the help of Begum Hamida Habibullah. SEWA started initially in the premises of Begum Hamida Habibullah's house.[69]

The girls from these poor Muslim families are now educated and are earning members of their families, a situation unthinkable for these families about twenty years ago. Girls after Intermediate classes have gone on to the University and taken up jobs. Most of them have taken up teaching as a profession. The Begum mentions one girl she met in London, who, after completing her Medical education (after passing the Intermediate examination from Taleemgah-e-Niswan), has settled in London.

The Taleemgah-e-Niswan is a Hindi medium school, where Urdu and Arabic are taught and Urdu is a compulsory subject till class VI. The School offers Arabic, among other subjects, as a Board subject in class XII. The girls are also taught to read the Quran. Two teachers are hired to teach the girls how to read the Quran and their salary is paid by Abdul Razzak, an advocate. Every year 60 girls complete the Quran and are awarded prizes.

Notwithstanding its meager resources, the College provides physical education to its students. It boasts of a Volley Ball team that has won prizes of considerable sum from the government at district-level competitions. Basket Ball, Badminton and Table Tennis are also played.[70]

Two units of Girl Guides function in the College. Camps are regularly organized. The teams have participated in District and State level rallies and received commendable positions. The Red Cross Society also functions actively and undertakes various activities.

The Talibat Imdadi Fund helps the poor students by donating books and clothes.

The Parents' and Teachers' Association has also helped the College to the tune of thousands of rupees by donating furniture and conducting repairs in the College.

Government Khursheed Girls' Intermediate College, Rampur

The education of Muslim boys and girls in northern India was given a fillip only after the rise of the Aligarh Movement. But even after that initial spurt the institutions for the education of Muslim girls were very inadequate. This holds true for all regions of the country. There were some arrangements for girls' education in the States of Hyderabad, Awadh, Bhopal and other States that had Muslim rulers.

In Rampur, when Nawab Sir Syed Raza Ali Khan took on the reins of administration, there was only one school in the entire Rampur State, comprising Classes 4 to 9, where the Quran and Arabic and Persian languages were taught. This school was meant for boys only. The students had to appear for the High School examination from Bareilly College, Bareilly. Given this situation with regard to education of even boys, the question of formal education for girls did not arise.

Nawab Sir Syed Raza Ali Khan, who set up various departments for the benefit of the State of Rampur and appointed experts for each of them, was interested in education from the very beginning of his career. During his tenure some decisions were taken regarding education of boys along with girls, which augured well for the future.

Known for his modern outlook, the Nawab paid special attention to providing modern education to both boys and girls. An Educational Board was established to tackle the problem of education and its progress in a planned manner. Nawab Murtaza Ali Khan, the crown prince, was made the Education Minister of the State. Khwaja Ghulam us Sayadain, a prominent expert in the field of education, was appointed Advisor on educational matters of the State. He did immense good work for the promotion of education in the State.

From 1936, permission was given for the admission of girls in the Vernacular, Anglo-Vernacular and Middle schools that were established as part of this endeavour. While 200 primary schools were opened, in every Tehsil headquarter, a girls' school was established.[71] In 1932 a large girls' school was started in Rampur city in the huge building of Kotwali. The Primary girls' school was named Qamar Laqqa School and the new Lower-Middle school was named Raza High school.[72] In 1939, under the Presidentship of the Chief Justice of the State, Irshadullah Khan, an Educational Society was established. Centres were set up in the city and rural areas. Prof. Ali Ahmad Suroor and Prof. Abdul Shakoor and other such educational experts were appointed as guardians. In 1941, a school situated in the campus of Raza Textiles was opened in the name of his youngest son Nawabzada Baqar Ali Khan. It was the first co-educational school established by the government. Buildings for schools were constructed or arranged by the State. In 1945, a Model Montessori School was established which was a co-educational institution. Trained and cultured teachers and lecturers were appointed. In 1943-44, 21 centres of education were further opened in the rural areas. Night schools were opened for private students. All the educational centres and night schools had facility for education of girls too. In 1943-44, the strength of all the recognized schools was about 12,000.[73] In 1945, primary education was made compulsory and Urdu was declared to be the State language.[74]

Scholarships were to be given for higher education.[75]

On 20th April, 1932, on the birth of his first daughter, Nawabzadi Khursheed Laqa Begum alias Muneer Jahan Begum alias Don Bibi, the Nawab established a school for girls and named it after his daughter as Khursheed Girls' School. Mrs. Zaka was appointed as the first headmistress. On 7th December, 1932, the School was inaugurated by Her Highness Nawab Rafat Zamani Begum. The strength of the School in the first year was 150 students belonging to both communities. Initially, the School was started in a large building of Khusro Bagh, but later in 1947, when the co-educational Raza Degree college was established there, the girls' school was shifted to Iqbal Manzil and Khan-e-Khana Manzil from where it is still functioning. After the merger of the

Rampur State in 1949, the administration of the School came into the hands of the U.P. Government and it became an Intermediate College in 1953.

The establishment of the Girls' School by the Nawab had its own share of critics, and this time the criticisms were of a different kind. We have seen the kind of hostility and criticisms that the Abdullah Girls' College, Aligarh and Karamat College, Lucknow faced in the early years of their inception. The brunt of the criticism was aimed at the character of the girls. Criticisms never took the form of character assassination of the founders. Here we find the people of Rampur State casting aspersions on the character of the Nawab himself. There were a lot of criticisms and objections by people who said that the School was established for the pleasure of the Nawabs. Therefore, the Nawab vowed never to enter its premises himself and neither did he allow his sons to enter it. So delicate was the issue of girls' education!

In September1946, when there was some tension regarding the early Morning Prayer in Khursheed Girls' School, it was duly clarified in the Gazette of the State that the schools have been established for the Hindu and Muslim girls without any discrimination and that the religious feelings of all will be respected. The teachers were also from all communities without discrimination. Since a long time, the practice of recitation of the Quran in the Morning Assembly has been followed by singing of patriotic songs. The Hindu students appealed to the Headmistress that they be given permission to sing religious songs (*bhajans*). Her Highness and the Nawab, after consulting the local eminent people took the following decisions. It was stipulated that:[76]

- The Muslim girls would recite the Quran as usual before studies began.

- This would be followed by the singing of *bhajans* chosen by Ram Ratanji of the Education Department, by Hindu girls.
- All students then would recite a poem together. No political or religious matter would form any part of the poem. It would be approved of by the Department of Education.
- During school hours, facility was given for the performance of *Namaaz.*

In 1936, the 47th All India Muslim Educational Conference was convened in Rampur. This was presided over by His Highness Sultan Mohd. Shah Agha Khan and inaugurated by Nawab Raza Ali Khan of Rampur. The Conference was divided into four sessions. One session was dedicated to the Department of Female Education. Nawabzada Liaquat Ali Khan was made the President and Prof. Bashir Ahmad Hashmi the Secretary.[77] In this session a number of measures for the promotion of female education were accepted. The implementation of these suggestions gave a fillip to the education of girls not only in Rampur but in the entire country. In his historic inaugural speech the Nawab of Rampur highlighted the importance of female education by mentioning about the establishment of the Khursheed Girls' School, a shining example of the increasing awareness and sensitivity of the people of Rampur towards female education.[78]

Traditionally, the population of Rampur comprised, among others, the highly uneducated haughty Rohillas, who were against the education of women. There was no concept or visualization of co-education. Religious groups other than Muslims also thought along the same lines. Even among liberal thinking people, there was no tradition of women's education. At best, in few families, they were taught to read and write Urdu and Persian and to learn to recite the Quran at home. People thought that modern education would encourage bad manners and shameless conduct amongst women. This changed from the time of Nawab Raza Ali Khan who opened co-educational institutions, which was truly a revolutionary step for its times. Now there are an adequate number of schools in Rampur district.[79]

Saghir Fatima Girls' Intermediate College, Agra

The Aligarh Movement had awakened awareness and need for education among Muslims on scientific lines. As in other parts of the country, so also in Agra, indigenous efforts to educate Muslim boys gave birth to the establishment of Anjumans to create love for and awareness of education among the Muslims. The establishment of 'Anjuman Mohammedia' is a case in point. It was established in 1906 by Saeed Ahmad Marharwi in view of the lack of interest in the education of Muslims in Agra and areas around it. Through this institution, work for the social upliftment of Muslims was started. Helping the neglected poor children, helping the widows, burial of unknown dead bodies, women's education, etc. were its main work. In September 1913, Madarsa Mohammedia was established under the Anjuman in the Shahi Masjid Lashkar Khan, near the Kutchery. In due course, this Madarsa progressed and came to be known as the Shoeb Mohammedia Anglo- Oriental College.

Saeed Ahmad worked hard for the education of Muslims, and looked on the education of Muslim women as extremely necessary for the good of the Muslim community as a whole. He, along with his supporters like Shoeb Saheb Tonki and Sheikh Sirajudin Qureishi, promoted the idea that a girls' school should be established for the promotion of women's education. In 1918, under the banner of Anjuman Mohammadiya he organised a Conference of Muslim women to discuss the importance and need for Muslim women's education, in which around 200 Muslim women participated from Agra and adjacent areas. He felt that women generally had religious education but were wanting in secular education, as no school was available for that. In his speech he said that if the Muslims wanted the progress and welfare of the community, and to enable the coming generations live in peace and harmony, it was necessary for Muslim girls to be educated. He reasoned that it was necessary to establish a Muslim girls' school similar to the Shoeb Mohammadiya Boys' School. He compared education to jewellery and said that education was the real jewel that a woman must acquire. He encouraged Muslim women to extend their support for the establishment of a girls' school. A widow by the name of Saghir Fatima supported the views of Maulana Saeed Ahmad and there and then donated all her jewellery for the establishment of a girls' school. Saeed Ahmad was very impressed with this gesture and he established a girls' school in her name on 10th September 1918, which later came to be known as Saghir Fatima Mohammedia Girls' Intermediate College. This school has played an important role in educating Muslim girls. Established in 1918, the School became a Junior High School in 1920, a High School in 1945 and an Intermediate College in 1963. It obtained minority status in 1986.

(This information is based on an interview with the Manager, and also the article 'Mukhtasar Taarikh' in the College Diary 2007-08 of the Saghir Fatima Girls' Intermediate College, Agra. No other information regarding the school is maintained by the College.)

References

1. Khan, Hamid Ali, *Hayat-i-Maulana Karamat Husain*, Al-Nazir Press, Lucknow.
2. 'Sayyid Karamat Husain and the Education for Women' by Gail Minault in Violette Graf (ed.) *Memoirs of a City*, OUP, Delhi, p.155.
3. Khan, Hamid Ali, op.cit., pp. 14-16.
4. Ibid., pp. 20-21.
5. Ibid., pp. 30-34.
6. Ibid., pp. 36-38.

7. Ibid., p. 39.
8. Ibid., pp. 101-102.
9. Gail Minault op.cit., p.157.
10. Khan, Hamid Ali, op. cit., pp. 57-62.
11. Ibid., pp. 71-72.
12. Ibid., pp. 95-113.
13. Ibid., pp. 151-152.
14. Ibid., pp. 103-6.
15. Muhammadan Educational Conference, 1891, Resolution No. 6, p. 79.
16. Khan, Hamid Ali, op. cit., p. 107.
17. Minault, Gail, op. cit., p. 159.
18. File No. 332A/II/1905, U. P State Archives. In the Report of the Committee on Female Education that was subsequently submitted in May 1905, Justice Karamat Husain disagreed with the rest of the members as to the desirability of having separate schools for Hindu and Muslim girls even in the primary stage. He maintained that the separation of Hindu and Muslim girls at any stage was not only unnecessary but undesirable.
19. Rizvi, Saiyid Athar Abbas, *Socio-Intellectual History of Isna' Ashari Shi'is of India* Vol. II. Munshiram Manoharlal, 1986, p. 416.
20. Khan, Hamid Ali, op. cit., p. 111. Raja of Mahmudabad, Sir Muhammad Ali Muhammad, was active in Muslim political and educational causes, including the Muslim League and M.A.O. College, Aligarh. Cf. Francis Robinson, *Separatism Among Indian Muslims*, Cambridge, Cambridge University Press, 1974, p. 380. Impressed with the Crosthwaite School that Karamat Husain had helped found, he wanted to found a school in Lucknow exclusively for Muslim girls.
21. Khan, Hamid Ali, op. cit., pp. 159-161.
22. Ibid., p. 166.
23. Ibid., pp. 174-178.
24. Raja of Mahmudabad arranged a house on rent belonging to Chowdhry Nusrat Ali Sandile, a taluqdar, for opening the Muslim Girls' school in Lucknow.

25. Haider, Qurratulain, *Kar-e-Jahan Daraaz Hai*, Universal Litho Press Bombay, 1977, pp. 21-222.
26. U.P. State Archives File No.208/1913.
27. Khan, Hamid Ali, op. cit., pp. 161-163.
28. Ibid., pp. 163-164.
29. Haider, Qurratulain, op. cit., p. 221.
30. Ibid., p. 222.
31. Ibid., p. 223.
32. Khan, Hamid Ali, op. cit., p. 173.
33. Ibid., pp. 248-250.
34. Rizvi, Saiyid Athar Abbas, op. cit., p. 417.
35. Minault, Gail, op. cit., pp. 163-164.
36. Ibid.
37. Interview with Dr. Sabiha Anwar, Karamat Husain Muslim Girls' P.G. College, January, 2007.
38. Begum Khursheed Khwaja was the wife of A.M. Khwaja, Bar-at Law. Her father, Nawab Jung Hamidullah Khan and her father-in-law, Mohd.Yusuf, an eminent person of Aligarh, were related to Sir Syed Ahmad Khan and are among the founding fathers of Aligarh Muslim University.
39. *Souvenir*, Platinum Jubilee Celebrations, 2006; Address by the Manager, Hamidia Girls' Intermediate College, Allahabad.
40. Ibid.
41. Memorandum of Association and Rules and Regulations of the Association for the Education of Muslim Women at Allahabad, 2002.
42. Ibid.
43. Ibid.
44. Ibid.
45. Begum T.R. Shervani was the wife of Mustafa Rashid Shervani, a noted industrialist, running the Geep Industry in Allahabad.
46. *Souvenir*, Platinum Jubilee Celebrations, 2006; Address by the Manager, Hamidia Girls' Intermediate College, Allahabad.
47. Ibid.

48. Hamidia Girls' Degree College, *Annual Magazine*, 1983: Introduction, Rehana Tariq, Lecturer.

49. Dr. Mansoor Hasan is a noted cardiologist and has retired as Prof. and Head, Dept. of Cardiology, King Georges Medical College, Lucknow.

50. Information Brochure 2007; Hamidia Girls' Degree College.

51. Ibid. Also interview of Dr. Rehana Tariq, Principal, Hamidia Girls' Degree College, Allahabad, January, 2008.

52. Information Brochure 2007; Hamidia Girls' Degree College.

53. Ibid.

54. Annual Report of Taleemgah-e-Niswan, 1988-90; Editor Shakir Ali Siddiqui B.A. (Hons.), M.A.; M.L.C. (Honorary Manager).

55. Interview of Begum Hamida Habibullah, President, Managing Committee, Taleemgah-e-Niswan, October, 2007. Begum Hamida Habibullah is the daughter-in-law of Inam Fatima Habibullah, founder of Taleemgah-e-Niswan. She married the youngest son of the Founder, Lt. Gen. Enayat Habibullah. Inam Habibullah, the daughter of Syed Maqbool Hussain Alvi of Kakori, belonged to a distinguished scholarly family. She came from a family that were proud of being people of learning, and became judges and professionals. She was taught Arabic, Persian and Urdu at home. She married Sheikh Mohammed Habibullah, Taluqdar of Saidanpur and Vice Chancellor of Lucknow University. Inam Fatima wrote a travel journal *Safar-e-Europe* about her trip to England in 1924, was a social worker, a Muslim League activist and was elected to the U.P. Legislative Assembly in 1937. Her eldest son, Ali Bahadur "Sonny" Habibullah, married Attia Hosain, the famous Pakistani writer. See also Annual Report of Taleemgah-e-Niswan, 1988-90, and http://www.litencyc.com and www.harappa.com/attia

56. Interview of Begum Hamida Habibullah and Mrs. Shahina Hasan, the present Principal of Taleemgah-e-Niswan.

57. Interview with Begum Hamida Habibullah.

58. Ibid.

59. Ibid.

60. Annual Report of Taleemgah-e-Niswan, 1988-90.

61. Ibid.

62. Ibid.
63. Ibid.
64. Ibid.
65. Ibid
66. Interview with Begum Hamida Habibullah.
67. Ibid.
68. Interview of Mrs. Shahina Hasan, the present Principal of Taleemgah-e-Niswan.
69. Interview of Begum Hamida Habibullah.
70. Annual Report of Taleemgah-e-Niswan, 1988-90.
71. *Rampur State Gazette*, 14th September, 1946. Vol. I. p. 10.
72. *Akhbar Dabdaba Sikandri*, 18th June, 1941.
73. Administrative Report, Rampur State, 1932-45.
74. *Rampur State Gazette*, 15th May, 1948, Vol. II No. 28, p. 2.
75. *Rampur State Gazette*, 4th September, 1948. pp. 3-6.
76. *Rampur State Gazette*, 14th September, 1946, Vol. I. p. 10.
77. *Akhbar Dabdaba Sikandri*, 24 February, 1936.
78. Ibid.
79. Interview with Mr. S.S. Alam, Manager, Khursheed Girls' Intermediate College, Rampur.

Conclusion

The Muslim social reformers of the late nineteenth and early twentieth century were deeply concerned about "Muslim upliftment" and, as a part of this, Muslim women's education also became a focus of their attention. Perceptions of western influence, of the spread of proselytizing missionary activities as also the secular content of education, increased efforts on their part to develop an indigenous system of education for Muslim women, particularly as it was believed that they were the true preservers and protectors of their religion, culture and traditions, became their focus.

To some extent, the hostility to women's secular education in the nineteenth century was the result of an apprehension that women's honour, virtue and modesty would be 'compromised' if girls went out to schools, which in turn would lead to loss of cultural identity and cultural beliefs. Questions of women's liberation, gender equality and economic independence were never raised. Consequently, education of women was confined to the home or to religious education or to imparting basic skills like letter-writing and household accounting. People like Badruddin Tyabji, Sir Syed Ahmed Khan, Altaf Husain Hali, Rashidul Khairi, Mohsinul Mulk, Nawab Sultan Jahan Begum of Bhopal, Karamat Husain, Sheikh Abdullah, Syed Mumtaz Ali, Viqar-ul Mulk and others through their writings tried their utmost to 'awaken' the Muslims of Northern India on the issues of education, and some of them focused on women's education. The Urdu newspapers also contributed to creating an environment conducive for Muslim female education.

The success of the efforts made towards Muslim female education as epitomized by Sheikh Abdullah's efforts in establishing a school, its growth into a college and its integration with the M.A.O. College, Aligarh Muslim University, Aligarh, shows that the problems of women's education touched on the larger social issues. It was now a problem that was national in scope, and linked with social reform movements regarding women's lives elsewhere in the country, not directly and through shared perceptions, but in the concerns involved. Issues of honour, tradition, family values, role of women in the family were parts of all movements in the country that concerned themselves with women.

In this case, participation through financial aids or efforts to win public approval, as also to gain sufficient attendance came from areas that were widespread. A Boarding House for women (for example in Aligarh) necessarily meant that for the first time women were venturing outside their homes and participating in a process that with time would become more collective. The opening of the Boarding House enabled women from all parts of the country to live together and participate more fully in the process of educating themselves. Co-educational institutions and the State initiative for educating girls in Rampur meant essentially that a way was being opened for women themselves to become a motive force in the movement for their education. The more active advocates of women's education were convinced that it was the key to the advancement of the community in India.

It was, in this sense, an effort at 'modernity'. However, social acceptance and public approval, as also the values of traditional society were kept in view at every stage as both the religious and modernist groups primarily addressed the concern and needs of only the privileged Muslim strata. The perception of the Muslim leadership essentially was that women had to be kept away from the 'injurious effects of the Christian missionaries and also from the darkness of ignorance and superstitions'. As Ayesha Jalal says, a predominant feature of '*ashraf*' writings of the period on women, were the need for their moral uplift and separation from '*ajlaf*' women. Education was considered as a tool to protect the '*sharif*' women from coming in contact with the '*ajlaf*' while at the same time enable them to acquire the skills to discharge their role as wives, mothers, daughters and sisters in a manner befitting the expectations of a polite society.[1] The '*ashraf*' women were considered to be 'repository of tradition, culture and morality for the Muslim ruling class of northern India'.[2]

So '*Sharif*' values were perpetuated. In other words, care was taken to see that the accepted institutions of Muslim society were not seriously challenged. To do so would have meant the failure of their venture. The fear and apprehensions that a woman's honour, modesty and virtue could be at stake or was in danger of erosion was partly the cause of the hostile attitude towards women's secular education and boarding houses.

Their understanding of the problems involved in bringing women into the mainstream of national life, therefore, made them keep step with the changes in other aspects of their social life. They felt they should not proceed at a faster or more radical pace than they did. Religion in particular was not to be violated. All their concepts and actions were justified on the basis of traditional values. Perhaps these policies were necessary in order to secure social acceptance without which the schools would have failed. The need to segregate women under the garb of purdah was not only accepted as necessary, it was the essential norm. Purdah was never questioned, rather it was 'institutionalized'.[3]

The school was an extension of the family environment. It was like a home away from home. The study of the Quran formed an integral part of the curriculum, and Persian and Urdu were still emphasized. Though women were also trained as teachers, the main purpose of education was still traditional in the sense of educating women to become better wives and better mothers and homemakers. In other words, education was to enable them to adjust to the now more educated men.

'The overall stress was on domesticity and piety and status improvement through better schooling and appropriate literature'.[4]

Women's education therefore, was merely thought of as a means to enhance the skills of women to perform their traditional roles. It was not meant to open new avenues or opportunities.[5]

Unlike boys, education did not bring about an increase in the number of women gainfully employed in various professions. It was merely to perpetuate their traditional roles and maintain a continuity of tradition.[6] Since the Aligarh Women's College came to be identified with the '*ashraf*' in its early years, its efficacy in creating an intellectual awakening in the Muslim community as a whole in India is questionable. Moreover, given this traditional emphasis, even the Girls' School could not be publicly declared an ordinary school until 1910. The idea of an institution for women could not have been accepted until then, another factor which shows that the movement had at every stage to proceed in accordance with public approval.

Since Sheikh Abdullah and his family's focus was directed towards the genteel (*sharif*) society – a society preoccupied with social status and correct social graces and behavior – it weakened the impact of the School on enhancing the role of Muslim women in Indian Muslim society.

The education system, fostered by the Muslim leadership during these decades, therefore, aimed at furthering the emancipation of women only in a very limited sense. As such, some of its characteristic features, which have been discussed, would seem to us today very conservative. But seen within the light of the problems it had to contend with, as also the social system within which it had to function and which it eventually helped change, it was truly a radical step. For its time, it was essentially modern, and its long-term contribution to the emancipation of women in general is therefore considerable.

References

1. Jalal, Ayesha, *Self and Sovereignty, Individual and Community in South Asian Islam Since 1850*, OUP, 2001, p. 70.
2. Hasan, Zoya, Ritu Menon, *Educating Muslim Girls: A Comparison of Five Indian States,* Women Unlimited, 2002, p. 6.
3. Minault, Gail, 'Sheikh Abdullah, Begum Abdullah, and the Sharif Education for Girls at Aligarh' in Imtiaz Ahmad (ed.) *Modernisation and Social Change Among Muslims in India*, Manohar Publications, 1983 p. 231.
4. Hasan, Zoya, Ritu Menon, op. cit., p. 8.
5. Minault, Gail, op. cit., p. 231.
6. Ibid.

Bibliography

Archival Sources

I. National Archives of India, New Delhi

1. (i) Report of the Education Commission 1884.

   (ii) Appendices to the Education Commission Report 1884 of Punjab, Central Provinces, Bengal and Madras and United Provinces with Evidences before the Education Commission, 1882.

2. Selections from Education Records, Part II, 1840-1859, edited by J.A. Richey, C.I.E. published for the National Archives of India by the Manager of Publications, Government of India, 1965.

II. U.P. State Archives, Lucknow

1. File No. 332A/II/1905.
2. File No. 208/1913.

III. Documents from the Aligarh Muslim University Archives

1. Document No. 1/5.
2. File No. 51.Document No. 2.letter from the Hon. Secy, M.A.O. College, Aligarh, to the Manager, Peoples Bank of India, Limited, Meerut.
3. File No. 51. Document No. 3. Letter from Mushtaq Husain, Hon. Secy. to Sheikh Abdullah, Secy., Female Education.

4. File No. 51. Document No. 4.
5. File No. 51. Document No. 5. Letter from the Manager, The Peoples Bank of India Ltd., Meerut, to the Hon. Secy., M.A.O. College, Aligarh.
6. File No. 51. Document No. 6. Letter from the Manager, The Peoples Bank of India Ltd., Meerut, to the Hon. Secy., M.A.O. College, Aligarh.
7. File No. 51. Document No. 15. Letter from Sir G.A. Tayler, Agent, Bank of Bengal, Agra, to M. Mushtaq Husain, Hony. Secy. Mohammadan Girls' School.
8. File No. 51. Document No. 7.
9. File No. 51. Document No. 8.
10. File No. 51. Document No. 9.
11. File No. 51. Document No. 10.
12. File No. 51. Document No. 11.
13. File No. 51. Document No. 12.
14. File No. 51. Document No. 13.
15. File No. 51. Document No. 15.
16. File No. 53.
17. Proceedings of the Mohammedan Anglo-Oriental Educational Conference, 1886-1945.

IV. Proceedings and Reports

1. Annual Report of Taleemgah-e-Niswan, 1988-90; Editor Shakir Ali Siddiqui B.A. (Hons.), M.A.; M.L.C. (Honorary Manager).
2. Administrative Report, Rampur State, 1932-45.
3. Minutes of the Executive Council, A.M.U. 1925-1947.
4. Prospectus of the Muslim Girls' High School and Intermediate College, 1931-32. Akhtar Printing Works, Aligarh.
5. Qawaid, Muslim Girls' High School and Intermediate College, 1929.
6. *The Aligarh Institute Gazette*, 1886-1947.
7. *Rampur State Gazette*, 1946-48.

8. Report of the Mohammedan Anglo-Oriental Educational Conference, 1886-1945.The report of the Female Education Section since 1904 is important.

9. *The Development of Women's Education in India, A Collection of Documents, 1850-1920*, Edited by Sabyasachi Bhattacharya, Joseph Bara, Chinna Rao Yagati, B.M. Sankhdher.

V. Newspapers/ Magazines

Urdu

1. *Khatoon*, edited by Sheikh Abdullah, July 1904-1914.
2. *Tilism*, Lucknow, 24 April, 1857, No., 4. Vol. 1.
3. Aligarh Magazine, *Khawateen*, Aligarh Muslim University, Aligarh.
4. *Naiyar-i-Azam*, 1 May 1908.
5. *Akhbar Dabdaba Sikandri*, 1936-1941.

English

1. *Comrade*, edited by Muhammad Ali (1911-14).
2. Muhammadan Anglo-Oriental College Magazine, 1890-1940.

Interviews

1. Interview with Principal, Dr. Sabiha Anwar, Karamat Husain Muslim Girls' P.G. College, January, 2007.
2. Interview with Mr. S.S. Alam, Manager, Khursheed Girls' Intermediate College, Rampur, March, 2007.
3. Interview with the Principal, Hamidia Girls' Degree College, Allahabad, January, 2008.
4. Interview of Begum Hamida Habibullah, President Managing Committee, Taleemgah-e-Niswan, Lucknow, October, 2007.
5. Interview with Principal, Mrs. Shahina Hasan, Taleemgah-e-Niswan, Lucknow, August, 2007.
6. Interview with Mr. Jameel Qureishi, Manager, Saghir Fatima Girls' Intermediate College, Agra, April, 2008.

Other Magazines

1. Annual Magazine, Karamat Husain Muslim Girls' P.G. College, 1999-2007.
2. *Muslim Youth*, February 2006, Vol. XIX. Issue 142.
3. Souvenir, Platinum Jubilee Celebrations, 2006; Address by the Manager, Hamidia Girls' Intermediate College, Allahabad.
4. Hamidia Girls' Degree College Memorandum of Association.
5. Rules and Regulations of the Association for the Education of Muslim Women at Allahabad, 2002, Hamidia Girls' Degree College, Allahabad.
6. Hamidia Girls' Degree College, Annual Magazine, 1983: Introduction, Rehana Tariq, Lecturer.
7. *Kavish*, Magazine, Hamidia Girls' Degree College, Allahabad, 2004-08.
8. Information Brochure 2007; Hamidia Girls' Degree College.

Books and Articles

Abdullah, Sheikh Mohammad, *Sawanih-Umri Begum Abdullah*, Kohinoor Press, Delhi, 1954.

——, *Mushahadat Va Ta'ssurat*, Aligarh Female Education Society, 1969.

Aftab, Tahera, 'Negotiating with Patriarchy: South Asian Muslim Women and the Appeal to Syed Ahmad Khan', *Women's History Review*, Vol. 14, No. 1, 2005.

Ahmad, Imtiaz, ed. *Modernisation and Social Change Among Muslims in India*, Manohar Publications, 1983.

Ahmad, Mian Bashir, *Justice Shah Din, His Life and Writings*, Ferozsons, Lahore, 1962.

Ahmad, Nazir, *Mirat-ul-Urus* (Hindi Tr. Jain, Madan Lal), New Delhi, 1982.

Ahmad, Tufail, *Mussalmanon Ka Roshan Mustaqbil*, Delhi, 1945.

Ali, Mrs. Meer Hasan, *Observations on the Mussalmauns of India*, Vols. I and II, Idarah-i-Adabiyat- i- Delhi, 1973.

Ali, Maulana Muhammad, ed. *A Manual of Hadith*, Amadiyya Anjuman Ish'aat Islam, Lahore.

Ali, Moulvi Syed Iqbal, ed. *Syed Ahmad Khan Ka Safar Namah-i-Punjab*, Aligarh Institute Press, 1884.

Basu, Aparna, 'The Indigenous System of Education in the Early Nineteenth Century and its Decline' in Aparna Basu, *Essays in the History of Indian Education*, New Delhi, Concept, 1982.

Begum, Rehana, *Oudh ke Samajik Jeevan ka Itihas (1720-1819)*, Delhi, 1994.

Begum, Sultan Jahan, *An Account of My Life*, Vol II, trans. Major Abdus Samad Khan, The Times Press, Bombay,1922.

——, *An Account of My Life*, Vol. III, trans. C.H. Payne, The Times Press, Bombay, 1927.

Bhatnagar, S.K., *History of the M.A.O. College*, Asia Publishing House, Delhi, 1969.

Graham, Lieutenant Colonel G.F.I., *The Life and Work of Syed Ahmad Khan*, Idarah-i-Adabiyat-i-Delhi, reprint 1974.

Haider, Qurratulain, *Kar-e-Jahan Daraaz Hai*, Universal Litho Press, Bombay, 1977.

Hasan, Zoya and Ritu Menon, *Unequal Citizens – A Study of Muslim Women in India*, Oxford University Press, 2006.

——, *Educating Muslim Girls, a Comparison of Five Indian Cities*, Women Unlimited.

Husain, Mir Wilayat, *Aap Beeti*, Muslim Educational Press, Aligarh, 1970.

Hussain, Saleha Abid, *Yadgar Hali*, Anjuman Tarraqi Urdu–e–Hind, Aligarh, 1949.

Hausewirth, Frieda, *Purdah: The Status of Indian Women*, London, 1932.

Iraqi, Shahabuddin (ed.), *Sir Syed Ahmad Khan: Vision and Mission*, Manohar, 2008.

Intekhab-e-Mazameen Sheikh Mohammad Abdullah; compiled by Nadeem, M. (Alig.) and Siddiqui, Qasim Mohammad, January 2007, Female Educational Association, Aligarh.

Jain, M.S., *The Aligarh Movement*, Sir Ram Mehra and Co., Agra, 1965.

Jalal, Ayesha, *Self and Sovereignty, Individual and Community in South Asian Islam Since 1850*, Oxford University Press, 2001.

Kauser, Nasreen, 'Muslim Women's Education in the Nineteenth Century: A Study of the Traditionalist Attitudes', *Proceedings of the Indian History Congress*, Calicut University, 1976.

Kauser, Zeenat, *Women in Medieval India*, Patna, 1992.

Khan, Bahadur Sheikh Abdulla, *Biography of Begum Abdullah*. Trans. Atia Abid, Aligarh University Press, Aligarh.

Khan, Habibullah, *Hayat-e–Aftab*, Ishar Karim Press, Allahabad, 1945.

Khan, Hamid Ali, *Hayat-i-Maulana Karamat Husain*, Al-Nazir Press, Lucknow, n.d.

King, Ursula, 'World Religions, Women and Education', *Comparative Education*, Vol. 23, No. I, Special Number (10), 1987.

Lelyveld, David, 'Three Aligarh Students, Aftab Ahmad Khan, Ziauddun Ahmad, Muhammad Ali', *Modern Asian Studies*, April 1975.

——, *Aligarh's First Generation*, Princeton University Press, New Jersey, U.S.A., 1978.

Leonard, Karen, 'Women and Social Change in Modern India', *Feminist Studies*, Vol. 3, No. 3/4 (Spring- Summer, 1976).

Mathur, Y.B., *Women's Education in India, (1813-1966)*, Asia Publishing House, Bombay, 1973.

Metcalf, Barbara Daly, *Perfecting Women, Maulana Ashraf Ali Thanwi's Bihishti Zewar, A Partial Translation with Commentary*, University of California Press, 1991.

Minault, Gail and David Lelyveld, 'Campaign for a Muslim University 1898-1920', *Modern Asian Studies*, VIII, April, 1974.

——, *Voices of Silence: Khwaja Altaf Husain Hali's Majalis un-Nissa (Assemblies of Women) and Chup ki Dad (Homage to the Silent), tr. into English with Introduction, Notes, Glossary, and Bibliography*, Chanakya Publications, Delhi, 1986.

——, 'Sayyid Mumtaz Ali and *Huquq un Niswan* – An Advocate of Women's Rights in the Late Nineteenth Century', *Modern Asian Studies*, Vol. 24, No. I. February 1990.

——, 'Sayyid Karamat Husain and the Education for Women' in Violette Graf (ed.), *Memoirs of a City*, OUP, New Delhi, 1997.

——, *Secluded Scholars, Women's Education and Muslim Social Reform in Colonial India*, OUP, 1998.

Nurullah and Naik, *A Students' History of Education in India (1800-1947)*, Macmillan and Co., Ltd., Bombay, 1956.

Rizvi, Saiyid Athar Abbas, *Socio-Intellectual History of Isna Ashari Shi'is of India*, Vol. II, Munshiram Manoharlal, 1986.

Robinson, Francis, *Separatism Among Indian Muslims*, Vikas Publishing House, Delhi, 1975.

Sharma, S. Ram, *Women and Education: Women's Education in Ancient and Muslim Period, Vol. II*, Discovery Publishing House, 1995.

Siddiqui, Firdous Azmat, 'Muslim Women's Education in the United Provinces: A Case Study of Allahabad University' in *Muslims of Uttar Pradesh*, AMU, 2007.

Smith, Jane I., 'Women in Islam: Equity, Equality and the Search for the Natural Order', *Journal for the American Academy of Religion*, Vol. 47, No. 4, (Dec. 1979).

Smith, Wilfred Cantwell, *Modern Islam in India*, Minerva Book House, Lahore, 1943.

Stewes, Cora Vreede de, *Parda. A Study of Muslim Women's Life in Northern India*, Assen: Van Corcum, 1968.

Thanwi, Maulana Ashraf Ali, *Bihishti Zewar, Parts I-VIII*, Madina Book Depot, New Delhi.

Thomas, P., *Indian Women Through the Ages*, Bombay, 1960.

Tyabji, Musait B., *Badruddin Tyabji, A Biography*, Thacker and Co. Ltd., Bombay, 1952.

Zuberi, Mohammad Ameer, *Ziya-e Hayat*, Din Mohammd Press, Karachi.

Other Titles from Three Essays

Aijaz Ahmad, *On Communalism and Globalisation: Offensives of the Far Right*

Amar Farooqi, *Opium City: The Making of Early Victorian Bombay*

Angana Chatterji, *Violent Gods: Hindu Nationalism in India's Present – Narratives from Orissa*

Antoinette Burton, *Brown Over Black: Race and the Politics of Postcolonial Citation*

Archana Prasad, *Against Ecological Romanticism: Verrier Elwin and the Making of an Anti-Modern Tribal Identity*

AR Vasavi, *Shadow Space: Suicides and the Predicament of Rural India*

Arup Banerji, *Old Routes: North Indian Nomads and Bankers in Afghan, Uzbek and Russian Lands*

Ashraf Aziz, *Light of the Universe: Essays on Hindustani Film Music*

Badri Raina, *The Underside of Things: India and the World – A Citizen's Miscellany*

Barbara Harriss-White, *India's Market Society: Three Essays in Political Economy*

Biswamoy Pati, *Identity, Hegemony, Resistance: Towards a Social History of Conversions in Orissa, 1800-2000*

Brinda Karat, *Survival and Emancipation: Notes from Indian Women's Struggles*

Colin Leys, *Total Capitalism: Market Politics, Market State*

Daya Varma, *Reason amd Medicine: A People's History*

Deepa Ganesh, *A Life in Three Octaves: Gangubai Hangal and Her Times*

Eduardo Galeano, *Open Veins of Latin America: Five Centuries of the Pillage of a Continent*

Harsh Mander, *A Fractured Freedom: Chronicles of India's Margins, 2004–2011*

Jackie Assayag and Véronique Bénéï (eds.), *Re-mapping Knowledge: The Making of South Asian Studies in India, Europe and America, 19th-20th centuries*

John S Saul, *Development After Globalisation: Theory and Practice for an Embattled South in a New Imperial Age*

John S Saul, *Decolonisation and Empire: Contesting the Rhetoric and Practice of Resubordination in Southern Africa and Beyond*

John S Saul, *Liberation Lite: The Roots of Recolonisation in Southern Africa*

KN Panikkar, *An Agenda for Cultural Action and Other Essays*

KN Panikkar, *History as a Site of Struggle: Collected Essays on History, Politics and Culture*

Kristoffel Lieten, *Views on Development: The Local and the Global in India and Pakistan*

Meera Nanda, *Breaking the Spell of Dharma and Other Essays*

Meera Nanda, *The Wrongs of the Religious Right: Reflections on Science, Secularism and Hindutva*

Madhu Trivedi, *The Emergence of the Hindustani Tradition: Music, Dance and Drama in North India, 13th to 19th Centuries*

Meeto (Kamaljit Bhasin-Malik), *In the Making: Identity Formation in South Asia*

Mukul Dube, *The Path of the Parivar: Articles on Gujarat and Hindutva*

Omar Khalidi, *Khaki and Ethnic Violence in India: Army, Police and Paramilitary Forces during Communal Riots*

Omar Khalidi, *Muslims in Indian Economy*

Paul R Brass, *Forms of Collective Violence: Riots, Pogroms, and Genocide in Modern India*

Patricia Jeffery and Roger Jeffery, *Confronting Saffron Demography: Religion, Fertility, and Women's Status in India*

Perry Anderson, *The Indian Ideology.*

Pritam Singh, *Economy, Culture and Human Rights: Turbulence in Punjab, India and Beyond*

Radhika Desai, *Slouching Towards Ayodhya: From Congress to Hindutva in Indian Politics*

Rajesh Sharma, *In/disciplines: Notes on Culture, Politics and Education*

Ralph Russell, *Findings, Keepings: The Autobiography of Ralph Russell, Early Years, 1918-1945*

Ralph Russell, *Losses Gains: The Autobiography of Ralph Russell, Middle Years, 1945-1958*

RK Jain, *Indian Transmigrants: Malaysian and Comparative Essays*

Romila Thapar, *The Aryan: Recasting Constructs*

S. Irfan Habib, *To Make the Deaf Hear: Ideology and Programme of Bhagat Singh and His Comrades*

Shereen Ratnagar, *The Other Indians: Essays on Pastoralists and Pre-Historic Tribal People*

Shubh Mathur, *The Everyday Life of Hindu Nationalism: An Ethnographic Account*

Subhash Gatade, *The Saffron Condition: Politics of Repression and Exclusion in Neoliberal India*

Sunil Kumar, *The Present in Delhi's Pasts: Five Essays*

Sunil Kumar (ed.), *Demolishing Myths or Mosques and Temples: Readings on History and Temple Desecration in Medieval India*

Utsa Patnaik, *The Republic of Hunger and Other Essays*

Vasudha Dalmia, *Orienting India: European Knowledge Formation in the Eighteenth and Nineteenth Centuries*

Vijay Prashad, *The American Scheme: Three Essays*

Vina Mazumdar, *The Mind and the Medium: Explorations in the Evolution of British Imperial Policy in India*

Zaheer Baber, *Secularism, Communalism and the Intellectuals*